QUICK AND EASY QUILTING

Quick and Easy Quilting

by Bonnie Leman

Drawings by Mary Leman

Moon Over the Mountain
M.Q.M.
Publishing Co.

6700 W. 44th Ave., Wheatridge, Denver, Colo. 80033

To
George
and
Megan, Mary, Emilie, Georgianne, David, Andrew, Matthew

CONTENTS

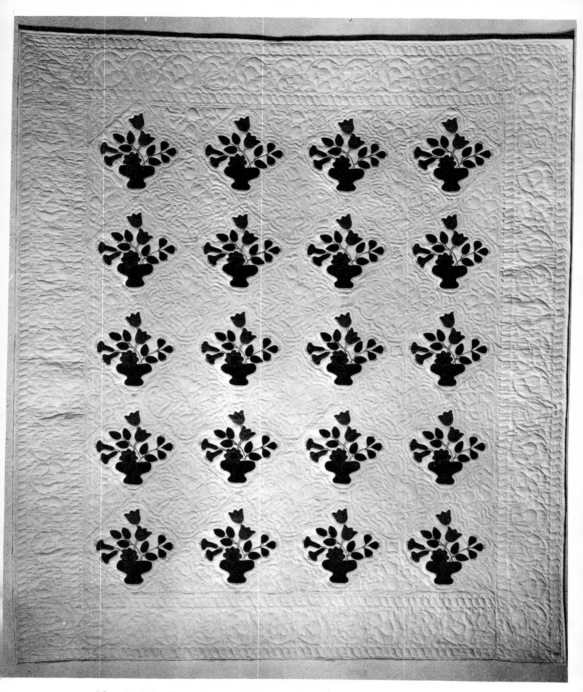

Plate 1. "Pauline's Bouquet," designed and made by Pauline Campbell of Ashtabula, Ohio. The quilt is made of appliquéd blocks and plain blocks, each quilted individually then set together. The pattern and instructions are included in Chapter 6.

PREFACE

When I set out to write this book I had a double purpose in mind.

First, I wanted to introduce an easy, modern way to quilt to women who have never tried this fascinating handicraft. As editor of *Quilter's Newsletter Magazine*, I get a lot of mail from women who would like to make a quilt but think it is such a large and complicated project it would not fit into their busy schedules. They are reluctant to begin because they feel quilting takes too much space, too much time, and too much trouble. I hope this book will show that quilting can be picked up and carried around as easily as knitting, crocheting, or needlepoint. Quilting is not a difficult or complicated needlecraft. On the contrary, it is one of the simplest to master. Anyone who can push a needle in and out of a piece of fabric can quilt. Any kind of quilt can be made with no equipment other than needle, thread, thimble, and cloth.

The large quilting frame seems to be an obstacle in the path of many prospective quiltmakers. They dismiss any idea they may have for making a quilt because they can't accommodate these cumbersome frames in their homes. I want this book to convince today's modern woman, whatever her age, that it is not necessary to use a frame when quilting. A whole quilt may be quilted by laying it on a tabletop or by holding it in the lap. A small quilt, such as a crib or youth size, is probably *easier* to quilt in the lap. Regardless of the size or type of quilt, many women prefer to work without a frame. Besides the traditional quilts which can be made without frames in various ways, there are novelty quilts that were never meant to be quilted in a frame. I hope that by showing potential quilters all these different methods, I can encourage them to take up this most satisfying needlecraft.

Second, I wanted to show experienced quilters a wide collection of methods of quilting without frames so they will have a greater choice of techniques. I believe that women who already enjoy the pleasures of quilting in the conventional way will be enthusiastic about learning new ways to pursue their hobby. It is always interesting and challenging to improve our skills in a favorite activity or field of interest.

It is not the purpose of this book to argue against quilting in the frame. What other craft provides the opportunity for six or eight women to work together harmoniously and companionably? The special satisfactions of sharing in this creative group project cannot be denied. Quilting bees are fun! The small quilting hoop is very practical and satisfactory also. I recommend it highly for any quilter who might prefer quilting in the frame.

My overall objective is to set down in one place complete information about still another way to quilt which uses no frames at all. To borrow a popular contemporary phrase, I wanted to "get it all together" for today's women so they would have a greater chance to find a method which is just right for them. It is my wish that, from such a wide variety of procedures, they will choose at least one and find out how enjoyable it is to make a quilt.

ACKNOWLEDGMENTS

My deepest thanks to everyone who helped me with this book. I thank George Leman especially for his constant help and encouragement, I thank Mary Leman who did the drawings, and the needleworkers who made quilts for photographing. An extra measure of gratitude is due the readers of *Quilter's Newsletter Magazine* who gave me ideas and suggestions—much of the material in this book I gathered through conversations and correspondence with them. I must give special mention to Pauline Campbell and Ernest B. Haight. These generous quiltmakers shared their techniques with me and sent me quilts to study and photograph.

Photographs. Plates 13, 14, 22, 23, and 29 by Roy L. Hale. All other black and white photographs are by Lloyd W. Rule. Color photographs by Harvey Dresner.

13

QUICK AND EASY QUILTING

1

Quilt-As-You-Go for Fun and Funds

Quilting without frames is not new. The idea of fastening two or more layers of material together for extra warmth or protection came before the invention of any kind of quilting frame. The ancient Chinese probably thought of quilting first. Europeans took hold of the idea about 800 years ago, during the Crusades. Although there seems to be no recorded date, the first simple frames were probably not devised until the thirteenth or fourteenth century. It was during this period that quilted clothing and bedcovers came into wide use to provide the warmth that was needed because of the cold winters in western and northern Europe.

Books which deal with the history of needlework in general or quilting in particular make little, if any, mention of the development of the quilting frame. It would seem that quilting has always been done both ways—with a frame and without—depending on whether or not one was available, and the preference of the quilter.

INTRODUCTION TO NO-FRAME QUILTING

During the nineteenth century in America, when quilting bees were the favorite social function of most families, the large frame became so associated with quilting that the two have become almost inseparable in the minds of many. However, right along with the quilting parties and church socials and women's club meetings that were happening around the large frame, lots of women were sitting at home in a rocking chair or on a settee, figuring out ways they could quilt in a more relaxed, individual way. Unfortunately for the image of quiltmaking, nobody paid much attention. Methods these quiltmakers worked out to quilt a block or small section of a quilt as they went along, or to fasten layers of cloth together without quilting them in the traditional sense, went mostly unnoticed in the flurry of organized quilting activities.

These techniques for making different kinds of quilts and for different quilting methods have been passed on by word of mouth, but very little has been published about them in book form. The McKim Studios of Kansas City, Missouri, one of the leading quilt pattern sources during the 1920s and 30s, published some patterns in 1932 which included a brief reference to the Block-by-Block Method of quilting described in Chapter 6 of this book. Most other published material about "quilt-as-you-go" (QYG) is found only infrequently in magazine articles.

It was probably the late 1940s or early 50s that saw an increased interest in lap quilting. Because quilting done in a large frame under tension produced such good results, the majority of quiltmakers didn't consider changing this reliable technique until our society became more mobile during and after World War II. Prior to this time most quilters stayed put and had a place they could set up a frame. When people began to move from farm to city and from state to state in increasing numbers, some quiltmakers either had to give up their hobby or find a way to do it more simply. Some turned to the individual standing frame; some discovered that quilting could be done quite satisfactorily by holding the quilt in the lap.

Other quilt-as-you-go ideas were also developed in the 1950s. The idea for the Nylon Puff Quilt described in Chapter 2 came into being after World War II, after nylon stockings had been around long enough for some practical-minded woman to save a bagful of discarded ones. She saw that these used nylons would make a very satisfactory stuffing for quilts—light but warm. Again, history is not clear, but the Nylon Puff was probably the forerunner of the Triangular Puff and the Hexagon Puff.

Some new improvements and innovations in quilt-as-you-go methods were worked out in the last year, some of them especially for this book. Chapter 3, for example, describes the Trim Method which is a new approach to solving the problem of how to join pre-quilted blocks.

Machine quilting is relatively modern. During the last quarter of the nineteenth century the sewing machine was the enemy of the quilt. Because of the Industrial Revolution, hand quilting was temporarily out of favor. Everyone wanted machine-made items. Turning away from machines and back to hand quilting became important to women in the early 1900s. After World War I, quilts were made commercially by machine, but most needleworkers tended to look askance at any quilt not handmade. It is only in the last two or three decades that *homemade* machine-quilted quilts have been recognized as having artistic merit.

Machine quilting at home didn't achieve any great popularity until the 1960s. It was then that women began to experiment with ways to handle big quilts on their machines. It was during this time also that new machines began to offer more and more stitch possibilities. Women accepted this challenge and discovered the creative potential of machine needlework.

ADVANTAGES OF NO-FRAME QUILTING

At least one of the advantages of quilting without frames is obvious. A quilting frame needs space—a standard frame about ten feet by ten feet if the quilters are going to be comfortable. Most of today's homes don't have that much room to spare. The individual standing hoop needs less space, but it is still too big to tuck away in a drawer.

If no frames are required, quilting becomes one of the portable needle-arts. It is easy to put a block or two into your purse for stitching while at the dentist's office or on the bus. All you need to carry with you is a needle, thimble, spool of thread, and a small pair of scissors, plus your prepared block.

It is much more restful to quilt while sitting back in an easy chair, perhaps while watching TV, than to sit upright at a quilting frame. Television or radio or conversation makes a perfect partner for quilting, a lovely way to relax and still do something with your hands.

If the quiltmaker is not limited by the necessity for frames, many more techniques and methods of quilting are available to her. For instance, ways to work with machine quilting may be explored.

Taking away the frames from quilting puts it into the category of needlework which can be done now, from day to day, at any time one feels like picking it up, instead of needlework which will be done "someday" when all the conditions are right. There is no need to wait until you can find out how to make a frame, or to get the proper boards or even to buy a ready-made frame. You could start a quilt right this minute without going to the store at all, because you must surely have some scraps of fabric in the house and an old blanket or piece of flannel you could use for filler. If you would prefer to wait a few hours until you can buy standard quilt batting, it is available in nearly all department and variety stores everywhere.

LAP AND TABLE QUILTING

Quilts from block size on up to double bed size may be quilted in the lap. Small-size quilts are more comfortable to handle in the lap, however. If lap quilting is to be used on a large quilt, it would be better to quilt it in four sections, then join the sections by the method described in Chapter 6.

In lap quilting the stitching procedure is somewhat different than in frame quilting. When the quilt is stretched taut in a frame, some (not all) expert quilters use two motions to make each tiny stitch. The right hand rests on top of the quilt; the left hand is placed below it. With the right hand the needle is pushed straight down through all layers; it is then pushed straight back up with the left hand. Anywhere from six to fourteen stitches per inch should be taken in this manner, the number depending on the skill and experience of the quilter. When the quilt is allowed to fall loosely in the lap, the needle should be passed in and out of it in a single movement. This allows the cloth to hump upward a little above the needle, which produces the slightly rippled effect characteristic of quilting. The hands assume the same sewing position as when a running stitch is to be taken in a single layer of cloth. Only one or two stitches at a time should be taken in order to keep the stitches short and of uniform length. The number of stitches per inch is usually from five to nine, depending on the thickness of the fabrics and filler as well as the experience of the quilter.

When quilting is done in the frame the stitches are usually begun on one side of the quilt, and as progress is made the

21

finished section is rolled under. When quilting is done in the lap the stitching should begin in the center of the quilt and work outward to the perimeter. This allows for any unevenness to be worked out toward the edges.

It is necessary to baste the layers of fabric and filler together whether frame or lap quilting. Perhaps a bit more basting is required for lap quilting. A long basting stitch in crisscross rows about six inches apart, plus a row around all four edges, is satisfactory.

Table quilting is done in the same way as lap quilting. One advantage of table quilting is that larger quilts can be accommodated more easily on a table. Lay the quilt flat on the tabletop with the sewing hand on top and the other hand underneath. Take one, two or three running stitches at a time, whichever works best for you. You will be more comfortable when table quilting if you sit on a stool four or five inches higher than a regular chair.

HOW QUILTS MADE WITHOUT FRAMES LOOK

Perhaps you are asking yourself, "But what do quilts made without frames look like?" The method you choose determines how the quilt will look. Some quilts made a block at a time look just like those made in frames. Other methods result in quilts which are unique and quite different from traditional quilts.

Methods Which Produce Unique Quilts

The novelty quilts and coverlets are discussed in Chapter 2. Each of the methods described in this chapter produces a quilt which is unlike any other. Most of these novelty quilts bear little resemblance to the traditional, hand-quilted bedcovers we associate with our grandmothers' heirloom quilts. Two of the methods for Pillow Quilt and String Quilt try rather successfully to imitate the look of old-fashioned patchwork. For the most part, however, each of these quilts has its own look and claims its own share of beauty.

Quilts Which Look Traditional

One of the favorite QYG methods is the Block-by-Block. We know this is not new, but how old it is exactly no one seems certain. The quilt pictured in the frontispiece was made by this method. It is difficult to tell one of these quilts from one quilted in the frame without examining the back. If the quilting design is elaborate, very close examination may be necessary to tell the difference.

The Hexagon Puff and the Triangular Puff Methods both result in quilts which are similar to traditional patchwork quilts. Instructions for these methods are given in Chapters 4 and 5.

The Trim Method of QYG described in Chapter 3 gives you the choice of using your imagination and creativity or trying for a conventional looking quilt.

Machine Quilting's New Look

Although machine quilting enjoys much greater acceptance now than it did ten or twenty years ago, the machine is still used more often for efficiency and speed than for the sake of beauty. This is not to say that machine quilting cannot be beautiful!

Some quiltmakers think that machine quilting is too symmetrical for real charm. Others say one can get a richer effect with greater depth because it is possible to use much thicker filler when quilting by machine. Machine quilting through one-inch dacron batting has a dimension lacking in hand quilting. It seems to be a matter of personal preference.

Many possibilities for machine quilting remain to be explored. The versatile darning stitch which is available on the newer machines has been adapted for machine embroidery and could quite probably be used in quilting as well. After you have tried some of the machine quilting suggestions in Chapter 7, perhaps you will want to experiment with some modern innovations of your own.

MINI-QUILTS

Needlepoint, embroidery, and other needlecrafts, besides being a personal expression of the artist, are primarily used to decorate, enhance, or add beauty to the things around us. Quilts do all of these things and have an extra attribute as well — they provide warmth. It is unfortunate that this limits the quilt's function. Because quilts are warm and have served traditionally as bed covers, most people think of quilting for that use only. Historically, quilts have been made for beauty and decoration as well as for warmth in bed.

However it is gratifying that some of today's young artists are using quiltmaking as a purely artistic endeavor. They use quilting as a means to express themselves because they like the wide range of color, texture and dimension. They are fastening three or more layers of materials together not for warmth, but to embellish or add dimension to the design of the top layer.

Quilts can serve many purposes besides covering a bed. Small-size quilts have many decorative and functional purposes. Specific uses are given in the following pages. In this book these small sized multipurpose quilts shall be called "mini-quilts" in order to separate them from bed quilts.

A "mini-quilt" is made of three or more layers of materials joined together by stitchery, in any size smaller than a bed quilt, and made for any purpose. The term "quilt" shall be used to embrace both mini-quilts and bed quilts. Mini-quilts are as versatile, artistic, functional, and beautiful as any other form of needlework — perhaps even more so because of their extra dimension. Just because quilts are most often bed covers, don't let that stifle your imagination.

For example, quilting need not be thick and puffy; it can also be thin and flexible. Three layers of cloth quilted together this way make perfect drapes for the living room. They are thick enough to shut out the sunshine and drafts, but are thin enough to drape well. If you use lightweight and light colored fabrics, the sun will softly filter through the drapes and highlight the quilting. If you prefer room-darkening drapes, use a dark preshrunk flannel for the inner layer.

As another example, quilts need not be square or rectangular; they can also be round. A quilted circle of bright patchwork makes a lovely accessory on a round table. Lay a round plain colored cloth on the table to skirt it and touch the floor. Top this with a mini-quilt which extends over the table's edge about four or five inches.

There are rooms in the house besides the bedroom where mini-quilts would feel at home. Other uses for mini-quilts in the living room are: small or large quilted banners, pictures, table covers, pads under vases or under art objects (designed especially to complement such objects), hassock covers, pillows, book covers, slipcovers for furniture, area rugs, piano bench pads, and lamp shades.

For the dining room you can make decorative mats for the buffet, pictures, hot plate pads, steak platter mats, coasters, jackets for glasses, bun warmers, tea tray mats, tea cozies, tablecloths, dining chair seat pads, and bell pulls.

Mini-quilts for the kitchen can be used as potholders, special beds for the pet dog or cat, toaster covers, mixer covers, blender covers, rotisserie covers, pads for receiving hot pans from the oven, curtains, window seat pads or cushions, kitchen posters, silver cases and stemware cases.

Ideas for the closet include pads for hangers, bags for sweaters or lingerie, shoe bags, sewing kits, pincushions, cosmetic cases, and wearing apparel such as caps, scarves, robes, jackets, pockets, vests, ski pants, belts, leggings, suspenders, foot warmers, purses, and tote bags.

For the bathroom you could make curler caddies, cosmetic cases, a cover for the hamper lid, tank cover, curtains, hosiery hamper, or a tissue dispenser.

Decorative mini-quilts for special occasions include Christmas tree ornaments, Christmas wreaths, and wall hangings.

Toys and games may also be made by patchwork and quilting. Checkers or chess are fun to play on patchwork, and these soft quilted "game boards" are perfect for children to take along when traveling or to use when they are confined to bed. An oversize quilted checkerboard would double beautifully as a beach or picnic blanket. Other toys which are easy to make for young children are balls and building cubes.

Directions and patterns for several of the mini-quilts mentioned above are found in chapter 9.

QUILTMAKING IS ECONOMICAL

Quiltmaking is perhaps the only needle art you can enjoy at little or no cost. Both appliqué and patchwork may be made from remnants of fabric on hand — outgrown or outmoded clothing may even be recycled. When the appliqué and patchwork are ready to be quilted, it is not absolutely necessary to buy filler.

Old blankets or remnants may be used for both filler and lining. If you prefer to buy quilt batting, the cost is only a few dollars for enough for a whole bed quilt.

This amount is low compared to the cost of wool for knitting, or canvas and yarn for needlepoint. Even if you choose to buy all new materials for your quilt, their cost compared to the value of the final product is very low indeed.

Many of the quilted items shown in Color Plate II were made with scraps accumulated from other sewing projects. Often not even new thread was purchased. If matching thread is not available, harmonizing or contrasting colors may be used in both patchwork and quilting.

QUILTMAKING CAN BE PROFITABLE

There is a renewed interest in handmade items of all types. Crafts are more popular now than ever. Strong evidence that many people are making and buying original designs is the mushrooming of handicraft shops everywhere. Even most department stores have added handicraft boutiques which offer quality handmade items.

Among the handmade items sold in these shops and in the larger department stores are quilts. The passion for patchwork has returned — perhaps even stronger than in the 1920s and 30s.

Several cooperatives have been formed in the last few years with the purpose of profiting from the current interest in quilts and patchwork. Among them is Cabin Creek Quilts of Eskdale, West Virginia, a cooperative organized by a VISTA worker to provide a source of income to the women from an economically depressed area. The members of this co-op turn out items ranging from pillows to quilts for king-sized beds. Another commercially successful co-op from West Virginia is Mountain Artisans, Inc.

Quilted items made by this group are offered in stores throughout the country. Patch Blossom Exclusives is the name chosen by the women of Tazewell County, Virginia, for their quilt and patchwork designs. The Freedom Quilting Bee, Alberta, Alabama, was one of the earliest organizations to improve the lives of its members through the promotion of hand-sewn products. Women from this group have appeared in many exhibitions giving quilting demonstrations, including the Smithsonian Institution's Folk Festivals.

Selling Your Quilts in Shops

The owners of shops and boutiques get most of their quilts from individual quiltmakers under consignment. Anyone who wants to make quilts for sale, either bed quilts or mini-quilts, has an excellent chance to sell them through these shopkeepers. A good quiltmaker can probably sell quilts faster than she can make them.

If you would like to supplement your income by quiltmaking, here is the way to get your quilts in shops for people to buy.

Label your finished quilts with their names, if any. Package each quilt in a large, new plastic bag so they will stay clean and look their best. Pin a tag to each quilt with your name, address, and phone number and the amount you want for the quilt. This amount must be less than you expect the actual price to the retail customer will be. Take the quilts to the shop owner, preferably at a time when he is not too busy, perhaps right after opening in the morning. Call the department store to find out if there are established hours for seeing new products.

If the store buyer likes your quilts and thinks they will sell, he will either buy them outright or take them on consignment, probably the latter. If he takes them on consignment, you will be paid when the quilts are sold.

To arrive at the retail price, he will add on the profit he needs to your asking price. The retail price will likely be one and one-half or two times your asking price. You should keep this in mind when deciding on the amount to ask for. (Retail prices on quilts vary from about $50 to $300, depending on their size, quality, and the location of the shop.)

You might also find an outlet for your quilts at local fairs and exhibits. Some communities hold these events annually at great profit to local quiltmakers. An example is the well-known Kutztown Dutch Festival held every summer in Kutztown, Pennsylvania. Last year well over 200 quilts made by individual quiltmakers were sold at prices ranging from $27 to $300.

Selling Your Quilts on Order

Another way to turn a profit from quiltmaking is to make quilts to order by customers on request. If you are an accomplished quiltmaker, word-of-mouth advertising is probably all you'll need to get a custom quilt business started. Tell your friends you plan to start taking orders and they will help you spread the word. You can also get orders by leaving your name with interior decorators in your area and by putting small classified ads in your local newspaper.

Sparetime Hand Quilting

There is always a great demand for quilters who will do hand quilting at home. Many women have quilt tops they have made or inherited, but do not have the time or inclination to quilt them.

You can advertise in your local paper, on bulletin boards posted in supermarkets, and in women's club bulletins or needlework magazines. Once the word gets around that you do hand quilting you probably won't need to advertise very frequently.

It has been customary for hand quilters to charge by the yard of thread used. A price of 2½¢ to 5¢ per yard is usually asked. A quilt using two 250-yard spools at 3¢ per yard would bring $15 for hand quilting. An average quilt would take from two to four spools of thread.

Some quilters prefer to ask a flat price depending on the size of the quilt and the elaborateness of the quilting design. This fee usually varies from $20 to $75.

Fund raising Through Quilting

For decades women have been holding quilting bees as a means of raising money for their church or club or favorite charity. While this practice never stopped, it has gained in popularity in recent years at the same time the craft revival was gaining momentum. Groups of women everywhere are raising money for their cause, either by hand quilting for a fee or by making quilts to raffle off or sell at auction.

HAND QUILTING IN GROUPS

If your organization or church group wants to raise some money and there are at least four quilters among you, you can be sure to get some of those needed dollars by holding a quilting bee.

At this writing, here are just a few of the many organizations using quilting bees as fund raising projects: Freeman Junior College Auxiliary, Freeman, South Dakota; Helping Hand Club of Stillwater, Minnesota; Women's Relief Corps, Platteville, Wisconsin; Methodist Quilting Circle, Gowrie, Iowa; Thimble Club, Gaines, New York; Mennonite Central Committee (Canadian Branch) Toronto, Canada; Carroll County Homemakers' Club, Westminster, Maryland; and the Park Temple United Methodist Church Quilters, Fort Lauderdale, Florida.

Plate 2. *Barn Raising, an antique quilt owned by the Colorado Historical Society. A quilt of this type may easily be finished by lap quilting when a blanket or sheet flannel is used as the filler. Quilting around each block is sufficient.*

Most of these groups expect the customer to furnish the finished quilt top, prepared lining, filler, thread and quilting patterns. The group marks the top for quilting, quilts, and finishes the edges.

These quilting bees may be held around the large frame at the club headquarters with four or six quilters participating. One quilt at a time is finished in this manner, in about eight to fourteen hours of quilting time. Or the bees may be held in members' homes in turn, with each quilter individually lap quilting or using a quilting hoop. As many quilts as there are quilters may be worked simultaneously. Each quilt takes approximately 40 to 60 hours quilting time.

QUILT AUCTIONS AND RAFFLES

Hand quilting for a fee is not to everyone's taste. Some fund raising groups prefer to design and make their own quilts to be raffled or auctioned, hopefully at a high price. These quilts are frequently designed with a certain community figure or event in mind. Quilts designed to commemorate local fairs or celebrations often bring excellent prices at auction. As this is being written, a few of the groups successfully using original quilts as fund raisers are: Mennonite Central Committee, Kansas Branch (auctioned over 200 quilts in April, 1971 for a total of $7,000); Detwiler Hospital Auxiliary, Archbold, Ohio; and the Old Campbell County Quilting Society, Fairburn, Georgia (in 1971 auctioned a commemorative quilt, depicting the county court house, for $500).

Does your organization include energetic members who are enthusiastic about selling raffle tickets? If so, they will find 32 many interested buyers when the winning ticket will redeem a beautiful handmade quilt.

2

Novelty Quilts and Coverlets

Experienced quiltmakers know that it is a good idea to make a sample block before starting a quilt from a new pattern. Sometimes patterns, particularly pieced patterns, may not fit precisely and small changes in the pattern pieces need to be made. Making a sample block also gives the quiltmaker the chance to try out a color idea before purchasing a quantity of fabric. For each of the novelty quilts in this chapter you would like to try, it is suggested you make a mini-quilt as a practice exercise. In other words, plan the size of your "sample block" so it will be an item you can use when it is finished. By doing so you will familiarize yourself with the technique involved; you will know whether you want to make a full-size quilt by this method; and you will end up with a useful piece of needlework.

Just as fashions in foods, clothing, furniture, et cetera come and go, fashions in quilts have changed from time to time. From 1870 to 1900 Crazy Quilts were all the rage. Appliquéd quilts were popular in the 1930s. Right now in the seventies bright patchwork seems to be the favorite. Most of the novelty quilts described in this chapter have at one time been either a fashion or a fad in the world of quiltmaking.

BISCUIT OR BUN QUILT

The Biscuit Quilt, also called the Bun Quilt, is made of small individual "biscuits" or "puffs," machine stitched together. It is one of the easier novelty quilts to make, yet one of the most attractive.

A Biscuit Quilt gives a decorator touch to the bedroom when used as a bedspread. Many other smart accessories can also be made using this method. Plate 3 shows two mini-Biscuit Quilts made into pillows. This pattern would also be very appropriate for hassock covers or window seat pads. Because they are so thick and puffy, these quilts can be slept *on* as well as *under*. When made of larger puffs they make perfect pads for young people to stretch out on to watch TV, or curl up in to read a book. A modern looking, comfortable sleeping bag could be made from one of these quilts folded in half with a zipper inserted along one side.

The technique for making this quilt has two variations. Variation I was used to make the pillow at the left in Plate 3. Large biscuits are used in Variation II, as in the pillow on the right in the same plate.

Variation I

The directions given here are for a quilt 67" x 85". The quilt is 27 squares wide by 34 squares long, each square being 2½" finished size. Of course, any size quilt may be made. These directions are for a two-color quilt with the biscuits pieced together in a checkerboard effect. You may use any arrangement of colors you wish. The yardage needed for a quilt of this size made in two colors is as follows: 6½ yards dark cotton (36″ fabric), 6½ yards light cotton, 4¾ yards white cotton for lining, 7 yards unbleached muslin for innerlining, and 9 yards bias tape for binding. You will also need a dacron quilt batt. Be sure all materials used are preshrunk, and wash and iron the unbleached muslin before cutting.

Step One. With a yardstick and pencil mark off and cut 918 three-inch squares from the muslin, 459 four-inch squares from the dark fabric, and 459 four-inch squares from the light fabric.

Step Two. Pin the corners of a 4″ square of cotton to the corners of a 3″ square of muslin as in Fig. 1. Fold and pin excess cotton into a pleat in the center of each side, always folding in the same direction. (See Fig. 2.) Before pinning the fourth side, insert a wad of dacron batting about the size of a large walnut. (Cotton batting and nylon stockings may be used also. If using stockings, cut about a 3″ width from the stocking for each biscuit.) Baste square all around as in Fig. 3.

Step Three. Make 27 biscuits in this manner, 14 from dark cotton and 13 from light cotton. Sew them in a row, right sides together, taking ¼″ seams and alternating colors. Press seams open. (After being joined with ¼″ seams, the biscuits are now 2½″ wide.) Begin and end the row with the same color. On the next row, begin and end with the second color. Continue making rows, alternating beginning colors, until you have 34 rows of 27 squares each.

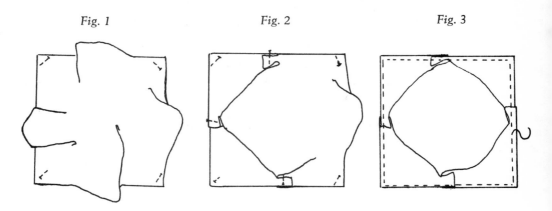

Fig. 1   Fig. 2   Fig. 3

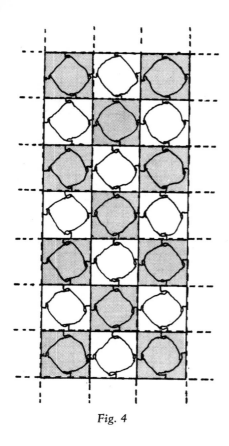

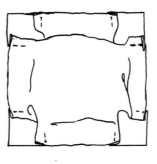

(Left) Biscuit quilt in 2½" squares

(Below) Another version of Step 2

Fig. 4   Fig. 5

Step Four. Right sides together, sew the rows to each other in crosswise seams. Press seams open.

Step Five. Prepare the white fabric for lining by trimming off the selvages. Cut and seam it so it will be the same size as the top. Baste it to the top, wrong sides together.

Step Six. Quilt on the seam lines between the biscuits, either by hand or by machine. Since the batting is not in a continuous **36** layer, this quilt is not bulky, and it can easily be quilted on the machine. The quilting will thus be done in 2½" squares. (See Fig. 4.)

Step Seven. Bind edges with bias tape.

Plate 3. *Two versions of the "Biscuit Quilt" made into pillows by Bonnie Leonard of Tangier, Ind. The pillow on the left was made of brushed velour in shades of orange, rust, and gold. Assorted cotton prints were used to make the pillow on the right.*

Variation II

This version of the Biscuit Quilt is made in the same way as Variation I with three exceptions: (1) The size of the square is increased. Instead of using 4″ squares of cotton and 3″ squares of muslin, use 6″ squares of cotton and 4″ squares of muslin; (2) The position and number of pleats taken in the top squares of cotton are different. The pleats are taken near the corners, two per side. (See Fig. 5.); (3) A larger amount of filler is needed for the larger biscuits. A piece about four inches square and two to three inches thick is required, depending on how full you want the biscuits to be. Dacron batting is the most suitable filler. Cotton batting cut this large would not keep its shape.

37

Fig. 6. Nylon stocking ready for insertion in "pillow"

PILLOW QUILT

The Pillow Quilt is also known as the Puff Quilt or Nylon Puff Quilt. Little "pillows" are made and stuffed separately, then joined. A section of a Pillow Quilt is pictured in Plate 4.

This quilt appeals to many homemakers because it is such an inexpensive but warm bedcovering. Nylon stockings that are no longer wearable are used as the filler. Using old nylons is really a very practical idea, because they make a comforter that is light-weight, yet warm and soft. If you want to use old pantyhose, just cut off the heavier part at the top. Use the leg portions in one quilt and the top portions in another quilt. Of course, you may also use cotton or dacron quilt batting as the filler if you do not have enough discarded nylons on hand.

Step One. Decide on the size you want your quilt to be. Figure how many 4″ squares (finished size) will be needed to make this size quilt. Cut *twice* this many 4½″ squares from the fabric of your choice. (For instance, if your quilt is to be 40″ x 60″, it would take 150 squares for the top. Therefore, you would need to cut 300 squares measuring 4½″, the extra ½″ being seam allowance.)

Step Two. Taking a ¼″ seam, sew two squares together on three sides, either on the machine or by hand as you prefer. Turn so the seam is on the inside. Take a nylon stocking and gather it up as you would when putting it on. Hold the toe part and slip it into the pillow you have made (Fig. 6). Place a pin through both thicknesses of material and the toe of the stocking. Turn under edges and whipstitch fourth side of the pillow.

38

Step Three. With doubled orlon or nylon yarn about six inches long, take a stitch through the center of the pillow where the pin is. Remove the pin. Tie the doubled yarn on the top side of the quilt.

Step Four. Make as many pillows in this manner as you need to complete your quilt. Sew them together with tiny overcast or slip stitches. If you wish, you may then add embroidery such as the feather stitch on the seams for decoration. Use embroidery thread the same color as the yarn used for tying, or you may want to use a single strand of the yarn itself.

Since Pillow Quilts are made from squares, the tops can be made in many different patterns. Arrange these squares in color patterns that are either traditional or modern as you prefer. Fig. 7 suggests a few simple color arrangements. Don't hesitate to mix different fabrics for interesting contrasts of texture, also. For example, bright-colored corduroy, linen and a nylon knit combined in one quilt top would make a contemporary-looking quilt.

Fig. 7. Six possible arrangements for Pillow Quilt blocks

 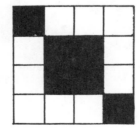 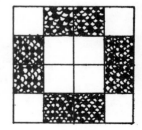

Plate 4. "Pillow Quilt" section, by author. Little "pillows" were finished individually, joined by hand with a whipstitch, then tied.

SHADOW QUILT

The Shadow Quilt is usually made of black velvet, flannel or other soft inner-lining, and satin in one light color such as white, pink, or blue. These fabrics are sewn together in such a way that the black forms a "shadow" on the satin, thus the name. Any other fabrics may be substituted for the velvet and satin. Today's bonded and knit fabrics are especially well suited to this old pattern.

The wall hanging in Plate 31 was made from dark red velveteen with a polyester-cotton blend in lime green, turquoise, white, royal blue, and lemon yellow. The vivid mosaic of colors decorates the wall as effectively as a modern painting.

Step One. Cut an equal number of 8" squares of velvet, flannel, and satin. Lay a square of satin on the velvet, right sides together. Lay the flannel square on top of all (Fig. 8).

Step Two. Sew together in a ¼" seam on three sides. Turn inside out. Turn edges of the fourth side and blindstitch closed (Figs. 9 and 10).

Steps in making a Shadow Quilt

Fig. 8   Fig. 9

Step Three. Fold two opposite corners in toward each other until they meet. Crease fold and open out square again. Quilt on fold lines (Fig. 11). Fold corners in toward each other once more and tack them together (Fig. 12).

Step Four. Finish more blocks in the same manner. Lay two finished blocks side by side and blindstitch together (Fig. 13). Add on other blocks around this nucleus of two blocks (Fig. 14), and keep adding on other blocks until the quilt is the size desired.

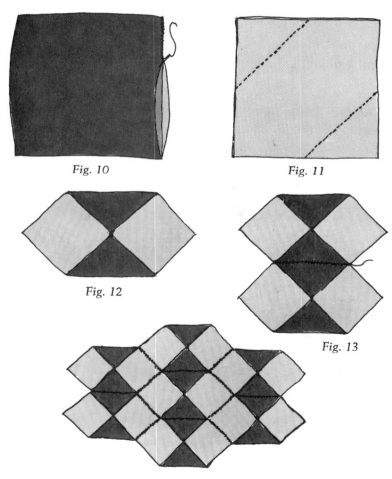

Fig. 10

Fig. 11

Fig. 12

Fig. 13

42

Fig. 14

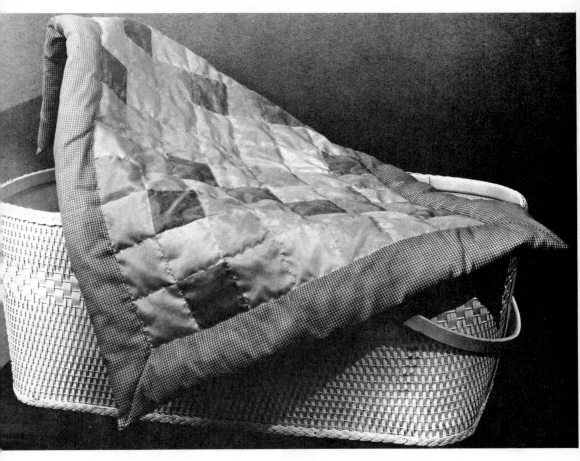

Plate 5. "Mirror Quilt" made for a bassinet by Mrs. Ralph Kerr, Arvada, Colo. The organdy which was placed over the pieced top before quilting was done gives this quilt a special look.

MIRROR QUILT

This novelty quilt, sometimes called the See-Through Quilt, is suitable for small quilts which can be worked as a single unit, such as a bassinet quilt. The finished product has a soft and delicate — yet elegant — look which is appropriate for a new-baby gift. Plate 5 pictures a quilt any new mother would appreciate.

.

Organdy is the material that makes these quilts unique. It is used as an extra top over the regular quilt top, and it serves a double purpose. Because it is semi-transparent the colors in the regular top are softened but still visible; yet it serves to camouflage any seams which may be in the regular top.

The Mirror Quilt shown in Plate 5 uses green-and-white checked gingham for the lining and border, assorted colors made into patchwork for the top, and white organdy for the extra top. The quilt is 27″ x 39″ and requires the following materials: 1-1/3 yard green checked gingham, 1/4 yard each of yellow, pink, blue, green, and lavender cotton, 2/3 yard organdy, and one dacron quilt batt 33″ x 45″.

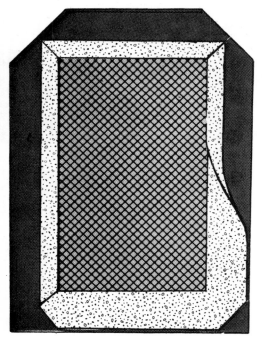

Fig. 15

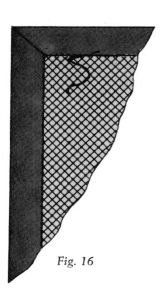

Fig. 16

Fig. 15 (Left) Assembling the layers

Fig. 16. (Above) Finishing the border

Step One. Cut the lining to measure 34" x 46". Cut seventy-seven 3½" squares from the assorted colors of preshrunk cotton. Wash and iron the organdy, and cut it to measure 21½" x 33½".

Step Two. Taking ¼" seams, sew seven of the squares together in a row. Make ten more rows of seven squares each. Sew the rows together to form a rectangle 21½" x 33½". Press seams in one direction (no need to press them open).

Step Three. Lay the piece of lining wrong side up on a table. Center the piece of batting on it. There will be half an inch of lining extending around all edges. Center the patchwork top on the batting. Lay the organdy on top of the patchwork. Pin all layers together at corners and sides of organdy.

Step Four. There will be six inches of batt extending beyond the patchwork top on all sides. Fold back three inches of this to form a double thickness of filler in the border. (Quilts have a special rich look if the border is puffier than the body of the quilt.) Cut out the excess triangle of filler which forms at each corner. Cut a triangle from each corner of the gingham lining so the corners may be mitered. (See Fig. 15.) Turn under the edges of the lining ½". Fold lining over the double thickness of batting. The lining forms a three-inch border and will cover the marginal ¼ inch of the patchwork and organdy tops. Miter the corners of the lining. Slip-stitch the border in place over the edge of the tops (Fig. 16). Remove pins.

Step Five. With fine needle, baste all layers together directly on seam lines of patchwork top. These bastings will be removed as you quilt, but are necessary to hold the quilt together at this point. Pins are not satisfactory for holding the layers together because they tend to leave holes in the organdy.

45

Step Six. Hand quilt the top in 3" squares over seam lines. Quilt also where border meets the top.

CATHEDRAL WINDOW COVERLET

The Cathedral Window Coverlet (Plate 6), has been around for a good many years, exactly how many no one seems to know. Small multicolored squares are sewn into "frames" of muslin

Plate 6. "Cathedral Window Quilt" made by Mrs. Charles Rutledge of Denver, Colo. Mrs. Rutledge chose to use a pale blue fabric combined with harmonizing blue prints rather than the traditional muslin and multicolored prints.

resulting in the stained glass effect that probably gave this quilt its name. The instructions which follow are for a simplified and up-dated technique for making this popular design.

For a 12″ square unit you will need ⅞ yard of 42″–45″ permanent press unbleached muslin or other fabric which does not need ironing to be relatively wrinkle-free. To figure the yardage needed for a coverlet, multiply ⅞ yard by the number of 12″ units required to make the size desired. For example, a 36″ × 48″ coverlet would require 12 units set three across and four down, and would take (⅞ × 12) or 10½ yards. You will also need 18 2½″ squares per coverlet unit for the "windows," or 12 squares for a pillow top only. Wash and iron all fabrics. Tear 9″ squares of muslin. (Tearing results in squares which are on grain.)

Step One. (Refer to Fig. 17.) Fold one of these squares in half and sew ¼″ seam across both ends. Put your index fingers inside the rectangle at points A and B. Pull outward with each hand, bringing points C and D together. Let the piece fall naturally into a triangle. Sew a ¼″ seam across the top, leaving an opening in the center.

Step Two. (Fig. 18) Turn right side out through the opening. You now have a square with seams on the inside. Press flat. Blind stitch opening closed. Fold the four corners toward the center so they meet. Press. You now have four creases. These creases are the seam markings. Prepare eight more squares the same way.

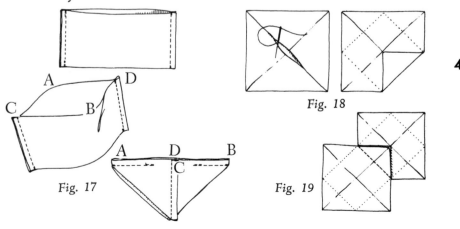

Fig. 17

Fig. 18

Fig. 19

47

Step Three. Lay two squares together, seamless sides touching. Seam across one corner on crease marks, as in Fig. 19, either by hand or machine. Sew three more squares to the remaining corners of central square in same manner. Press flaps down, and tack with hand stitching at corners which fall within gray area of Fig. 20.

Step Four. (Refer to Fig. 21.) Place a 2½" square of print over one seam. Fold back one loose edge of each flap surrounding it. This will cover the raw edges of the print square. Blind stitch these folded edges down. This is your first "window." Finish three more windows.

Step Five. Add four more prepared muslin squares at the corners of this piece, seaming them on the flaps which are not tacked down. Lay down eight more windows to cover the resulting seams, and finish as before. See Fig. 22.

You now have a 12" square nucleus from which to build outward, adding on more squares in the same manner until you have the size you want. If you want a pillow top, you can stop at this point. For a coverlet, construct it in 12" square units, such as this one, then join them by seaming the perimeter flaps.

48

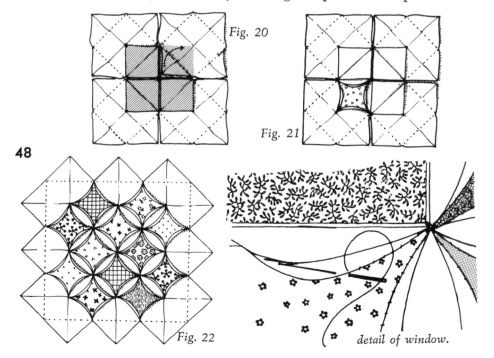

Fig. 20

Fig. 21

Fig. 22

detail of window.

Button Quilt

To make this variation of the Cathedral Window, sew "buttons" over the corners where the colored squares meet. These buttons are simply two-inch circles of fabrics which are filled with a cotton ball and then gathered up around the edges. Plate 7 shows a close-up of a Button Quilt.

Plate 7. "Button Quilt," a variation of the Cathedral Window Quilt, made by Bonnie Leonard of Tangier, Ind. The buttons serve to cover any imperfections there might be at the corners of the blocks.

Plate 8. *"Bon-Bon"* or *"Yo-Yo"* Quilt made by Doris Hannon, Lebanon, N. H. Mrs. Hannon tied this quilt where the circles are joined. This step gives the quilt added strength, but it is optional. A lightweight blanket was used as the lining onto which the gathered circles were sewn.

BON-BON COVERLET

A scrap quilt to be made as remnants accumulate, this unusual coverlet is painstaking to construct. It is made of many small circles of fabrics which are hemmed, gathered and tacked together in units or blocks. These blocks are then backed by a lining.

"Puff," "Powder Puff," "Pinwheel," "Bed of Roses," "Yo-Yo," "Rosette," and "Bon-Bon" are some of the names this coverlet has been called down through the years. When the circles are

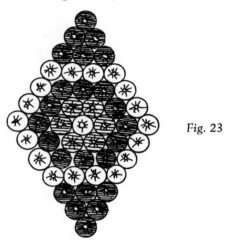

Fig. 23

set in a hexagonal pattern it is called "Martha Washington's Flower Garden." (See Fig. 23.) Most often these circles are set together in a hit or miss fashion, and sometimes the quilt is tied as shown in Plate 8.

Quiltmakers who might not have the patience or the desire to make a whole quilt by this method probably would enjoy making a pillow cover or small couch-throw. This old pattern is favored now in clothing and accessories as well as home decoration.

Step One, making the circles. From a printed fabric scrap, cut a circle 2½" in diameter. Turn under ¼" around edge. Take small running stitches in the fold and gather tightly. Polyester thread works well for this; make sure it is knotted securely at the

51

end. The finished circle will be about 1¼" in diameter. (Larger circles make for less work. The circles may be cut as large as you like. The finished circles will be about half the size of the original circle.)

Step Two, joining the circles. Lay two circles side by side with the gathered centers facing you. (This will be the right side.) Tack the circles together by hand, edge to edge where they meet.

Fig. 24   Fig. 25

Two ways of joining the circles

Add on other circles in the same way to make a unit about 10" square. Units using more than 100 circles are difficult to work with. Make as many units as desired for your quilt. The circles may be staggered as in Fig. 24 or sewn together in straight rows as in Fig. 25.

Step Three, lining the circles. For a full-sized quilt, a sheet blanket or colored sheet makes a good lining. You can also cut a piece of lining from muslin, or the fabric of your choice, the size you want your finished quilt to be. Seam two pieces together if necessary to get a lining large enough. Hem edges of lining. Find the exact center of the lining. Place the center of one unit of circles directly on the center of the lining and pin in place, wrong sides together. Pin another unit of circles adjacent to the first unit so the edges of the circles meet. Tack the two units of circles together and at the same time tack them to the lining. The tacking stitches will go through two adjoining circles plus the lining. Build out from this central unit, joining the units and lining them simultaneously. The last row of units to be added to completely cover the lining should be of a size that will allow the circles to extend beyond the edge of the lining about ½". The edges of the lining should not be visible from the top of the quilt. Hand sew these hemmed edges of lining to the underside of the outermost circles with an overcast stitch.

STRING QUILT

For decades the String Quilt has been used by economical-minded women who either needed or wanted to make something out of nothing. The term "string" originally referred to the long, narrow strips of fabric left over from cutting a dress or other garment — strips that would normally be too narrow to be of any purpose. The term has come to mean any scrap of cloth which is longer than it is wide.

Women have long made quilts from these "strings," sewing them onto newspaper so they could be fashioned into a quilt top. Somewhere along the line, some woman cared more about the beauty of the quilt top than its economy, so she used larger scraps and arranged them in a design. In this way several variations of the String Quilt have developed.

Variation I

Early versions of the String Quilt used strips so narrow that several of them had to be sewn together to form a pattern piece large enough to be workable, such as a triangle or square. The method most commonly used was to cut the pattern pieces needed out of newspaper. These paper patterns were covered with the cloth strips sewn on one at a time. The ends of the cloth strips were then trimmed off even with the paper pattern. After the quilt top was assembled the paper was torn away from the cloth. (Sometimes the paper was left in for extra warmth, but it would eventually disappear with repeated washing.) These string tops

Fig. 26. Spiderweb Quilt, an early String Quilt.

were then sewn onto whatever was available (usually a used blanket or the best parts of old garments sewn together). Directions follow for making one such old quilt called the Spiderweb (Fig. 26).

Step One. Each block in this quilt will be 11½" square, finished size. Cut a 12" square of newspaper. Cut it in half diagonally both ways to make four equal triangles. Each of these triangles will be a pattern piece. You will need four for each block in your quilt. (A quilt about 58" x 80" would take

54

35 blocks for a total of 140 triangles.) You will also need four of Pattern A for each block. Cut these from light colored cloth instead of newspaper.

Step Two. Put cloth cut from Pattern A in position on paper triangle and pin (Fig. 27). Seam strings one at a time on both sides of piece A until triangle is covered (Fig. 28). Trim off strings flush with paper pattern (Fig. 29). One-fourth of a block is now completed. Make three more of these covered triangles and sew them together to form one block (Fig. 30).

Step Three. Make as many more blocks as needed for the size quilt desired. Seam these blocks together in ¼″ seams. Tear away paper if desired.

Step Four. Lay your finished top over the lining you have chosen. The lining may be an old blanket that is worn but still usable, widths of cotton flannel sewn together, or you may wish to buy a new blanket for the purpose. The lining should not be so thick that it is difficult to hand quilt. Pin and baste the top in place.

Steps in constructing a Spiderweb Quilt.

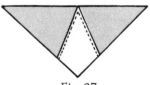

Fig. 27

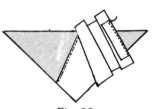

Fig. 28

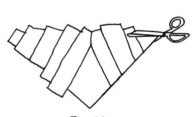

Fig. 29

Fig. 30

Step Five. Let the quilt rest in your lap and hand quilt through the seams joining the blocks. Quilting around the blocks is all that is required when there is no inner filling.

Step Six. Bind the quilt with a double thickness of bias cut from the same plain fabric used for Pattern A.

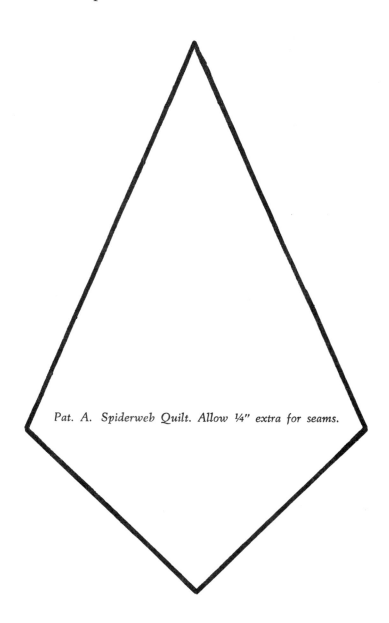

Pat. A. Spiderweb Quilt. Allow ¼" extra for seams.

Variation II

This version of the String Quilt offers you the chance to make an instant quilt. This quilt can be pieced and quilted an easy block at a time on the sewing machine or by hand. Although string quilts are traditionally made to use up scraps, don't hesitate to buy new material. One of these quilts is seen in Plate 9.

Plate 9. "String Quilt" made by Susan Ennis of Golden, Colo. Silk taffeta was used to create this modern version of an old favorite, in several shades of green with deep pink for an accent.

Step One. Cut four backing blocks 9″ square. A tiny calico print may be used effectively for backing blocks. Cut filler in four 8½″ squares. A sheet blanket, flannel, cotton batting or dacron batting are all suitable for filler. Cut strips about 1½″ to 3″ wide from the fabrics you plan to use for the top. The strips should be about 9″, 5″, and 3″ long. Lay one filler square on top of one backing square. Place one strip diagonally on the filler which is on the backing block. Pin in place (Fig. 31). On the right side of this strip, right sides together, place

Steps in constructing String Quilt, Variation II

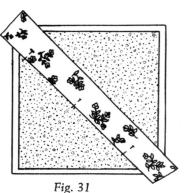

Fig. 31

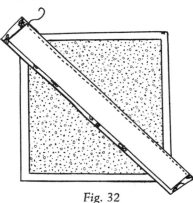

Fig. 32

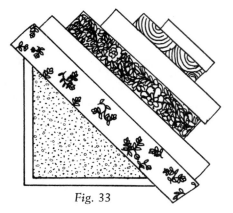

Fig. 33

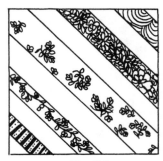

Fig. 34

Fig. 35

Fig. 36

another strip. Sew these two strips together in a ¼" seam, sewing through filler and backing (Fig. 32). Smooth the second strip out flat. Lay a third strip on top of the second strip right sides together, and seam as before. Continue sewing strips on until you reach the corner (Fig. 33). Repeat the same process on the other side of the center strip. Trim all strips flush with the backing block (Fig. 34). Make three more blocks in the same manner.

Step Two. Place the four finished blocks together so the strips form a herringbone effect. Seam the blocks together with ¼" seams on the wrong side (Fig. 35). Trim seams if necessary.

Step Three. Cover seams which are on the back of the quilt with bias tape or bias seam tape. Sew bias tape on with an invisible hemming stitch (Fig. 36). (The bias tape may be sewn on by machine, but the hand sewing yields a better looking quilt.)

Step Four. Make as many units of four blocks as you need to complete a quilt the size you desire.

59

Step Five. Join the units in horizontal rows. Four units placed side-by-side make a quilt 72" wide. Cover the seams with bias tape on the wrong side as you go.

Step Six. Join two horizontal rows of units. The seam to be covered with tape will go across the width of the quilt, and no raw ends of tape will ever be visible. Add another row of units, and continue adding rows of units until the quilt is the length you want. Bind all around the edges with matching bias tape in a 1″ width.

Variation III

A new interpretation of the String Quilt idea is illustrated in Plate 10. The technique used in this particular quilt is especially satisfactory for bonded woolen and bonded knit scraps. These fabrics do not ravel easily, so it is unnecessary to turn under the edges of the scraps when joining them. Some of the knits used in the quilt in Plate 10 were not bonded, and they tended to stretch at the edges giving the quilt a slightly uneven appearance. Bonded knits are probably preferable for use in quilts, at least for those made by machine.

This quilt is made of three units, each the length of the quilt. Each unit is small enough so that it is easily handled during machine sewing. The direction of the strips is planned so the units may be joined without any visible seams.

Step One. Decide on the size quilt desired, and divide the width into approximate thirds. Let us say you want a quilt 50″ x 80″. Plan the center unit (B) to be 18″ wide, and the two side units (A) to be 17″ wide. The length of each unit will be 80″.

60

Plate 10. (Opposite) "String Quilt," designed by author and made in sections with zigzag stitch on the sewing machine by Jane Younger of Lakewood, Colo. This quilt is made of woolens and knits in several shades of purple and lavender with white for contrast.

Step Two. Buy a length of fabric for the lining such as flannel, corduroy, homespun, or cotton. Slick-surfaced fabrics are not recommended. Cut three pieces of lining the same size as the planned units, adding ½″ to each side unit (A) for seam allowance. For a 50″ x 80″ quilt the lining for side units (A) would be 17½″ x 80″, and for unit (B) 18″ x 80″.

Step Three. Cut strips of bonded fabrics nine inches long and of various widths. Place one of these strips along the end of one lining unit (A) in the position illustrated by Fig. 37. (The extra ½″ of lining of the right side of the unit is for seam allowance.) Lay another strip alongside the first, slightly overlapping them. Sew the second strip down with a close zigzag stitch (Fig. 38). Add another strip and sew it down the same way. Repeat until the center division of the unit is covered.

Step Four. Cut strips of bonded fabrics 4″ wide and of various lengths. With the zigzag stitch piece a number of these strips to-

Steps in the construction of the String Quilt, Variation III

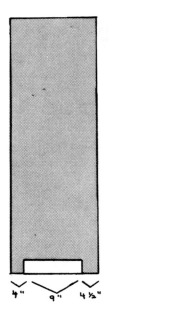

4″   9″   4½″

Fig. 37   Fig. 38

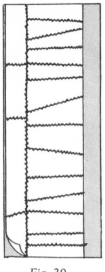

Fig. 39

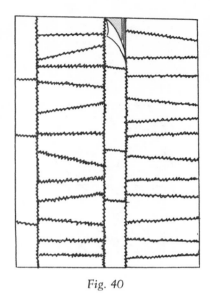

Fig. 40

gether end to end, to form a strip 80″ long. Lay this long strip on the left side of unit (A), and zigzag it down over the ends of the strips in the middle (Fig. 39). Do not sew down the outside edge of the strip. Make another 80″ strip like the first, and sew it down to the right side of unit (A). The ½″ seam allowance on the lining will extend beyond this second strip. Repeat steps three and four to make a second unit (A).

Step Five. Cut strips of bonded fabrics 18″ long and of various widths. Beginning at one end of unit (B), lay these strips on the lining and sew them down in the same way as above.

Step Six. Join the first unit (A) to unit (B) as follows: Lay back the 80″ side strip on unit (A) and seam just the lining portion in a ½″ seam to unit (B). The seam will be on top of the quilt. (See Fig. 40.) Flatten the two units out and press the seam under the 80″ side strip. Zigzag down the edge of the side

63

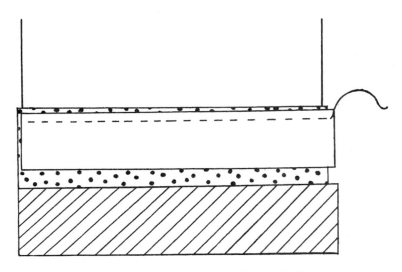

Fig. 41. Seaming cotton strips for String Quilt

strip over unit (B). Join the second unit (A) to the other side of unit (B) in the same way.

Step Seven. Bind the edges of the quilt with velvet, or the fabric of your choice. You will need one-half yard of fabric cut into 1½″ bias strips for this binding.

It is suggested that if you want to make this quilt out of cotton or some other fabric thinner than wool, use an inner lining such as a sheet blanket. You could make this quilt with a straight machine stitch, instead of a zigzag stitch, by seaming the strips together as in Fig. 41.

Color Plate I. *Biscuit or Bun pillow in plain colors. Moon Flowers pillow, corduroy pillow, Biscuit pillow in printed fabrics.*

Color Plate II. Martha Washington Star tote, pair of knee warmers, quilted cap, small pentagon ball, quilted vest, potholder, knee warmer with ties, Sunflower tote, knee warmer, two small pincushions, pot holder, Star Spangled Banner tote.

3

Trim Method

The Trim Method is a technique used to cover, camouflage or enhance the joining seams of pre-quilted blocks. The quilt top is made in individual blocks. Each block is quilted to a lining square of the same size, with filler in between the block and square. The basic idea behind this method of constructing a quilt is to sew these quilted blocks together before finishing the raw edges. The raw edges are then covered with decorative trim of some kind. The trim or stitching used to cover the raw edges of the blocks becomes a decorative element of the quilt. (See Fig. 42.)

There are several kinds of quilt blocks which lend themselves particularly well to this treatment. Appliquéd blocks are set off quite nicely by a "frame" of braid, bias tape, embroidery, or numerous other trims. Plain blocks made of one shade of a favorite color and quilted with an elaborate design are also enhanced by a frame of colorful braid at their joinings. Large squares of various print and plain fabrics can be pre-quilted, then

65

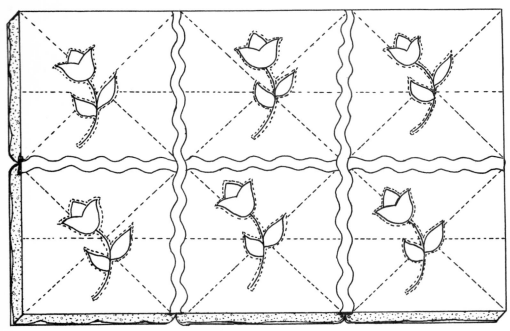

Fig. 42. *Pre-quilted blocks seamed together with rickrack covering the seams*

joined effectively with this method. Embroidered quilt blocks are obviously suited to this technique. Embroidery motifs from the blocks can be repeated in a row, or rows, along the seam line.

Pieced blocks, on the other hand, do not look their best joined by the Trim Method. The design of most pieced blocks is already strong enough without adding further design on the joining seams.

This chapter will show three basic variations of the Trim Method you can choose to suit your own talents and preferences.

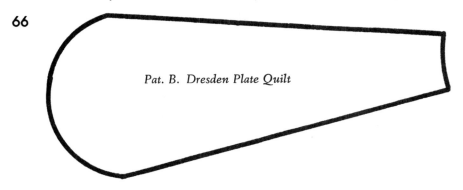

Pat. B. Dresden Plate Quilt

The blocks are 14″ square. For a quilt 56″ x 84″ you will need twenty-four blocks (four blocks wide by six blocks long).

Step One. Cut twenty-four 14″ squares of pale pink fabric for the top and twenty-four 14″ squares of white fabric for the lining. Cut twenty-four 14″ squares of dacron batting for filler.

Plate 11. Section of "Dresden Plate Quilt" made by Bonnie Leonard, from the author's design. "Dresden Plate" is a traditional quilt pattern usually made from scraps of prints, joined with strips between the blocks. This quilt shows how an old pattern may be updated by a quilt-as-you-go method. The color scheme is pinks and reds.

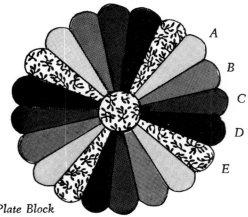

Fig. 43. Dresden Plate Block

Step Two. Trace pattern piece B. Glue tracing to piece of stiff paper. Cut out on traced line. Place this pattern on fabric and mark around it with pencil. This pencil line will be your seam line. Cut out ¼″ from this marked seam line. Mark and cut out ninety-six pieces of *each* of the following colors: (A) light pink, (B) medium pink, (C) medium dark pink, (D) dark pink, and (E) pink print. (You will need four each of these colors for every block.)

Step Three. Sew these pieces together as illustrated in Fig. 43. Press.

Step Four. Cut out twenty-four 4″ circles of print (E), one for every block. Lay one of these circles in the exact center of a 14″ square of pale pink. Position the pieced "Dresden Plate" over this circle. Turn under raw edges of Plate on marked line, pin and baste. Appliqué the Plate onto the square. Appliqué twenty-three more blocks in the same manner.

Step Five. Mark each block for quilting as shown in Fig. 44. Sandwich filler between lining square and appliquéd block, pin and baste. Hand quilt each block.

Step Six. Cut 1½″ wide bias strips from pink print (E). Turn under both edges of bias strips so finished strip is ¾″ wide. Press.

Step Seven. Seam two blocks together to make a unit, lining sides touching, so the seam will be on top of block. Seam two

68

more blocks together for another unit. Trim seams close, and baste seam down to one side. Seam one unit to the other unit in the same way. Trim seams and baste down. Cover the horizontal seam with bias strip. Blind stitch bias down by hand. Now cover crossing seam in the same way. (See Plate 11.)

Step Eight. Make five more units. Join the units side by side, to form a section four blocks wide by two blocks deep. Make two more sections. The sections are joined just as the blocks and units are joined. The last seams will be two crosswise seams which will be covered with bias strips the width of the quilt.

Step Nine. Bind all edges with the pink print bias strips.

Fig. 44. Quilting design for Dresden Plate Quilt

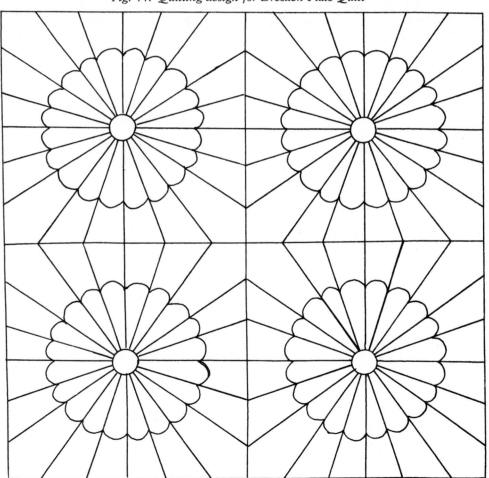

Plate 12. Two pale yellow squares, hand quilted with a simple tulip design, then joined by machine with seam on top. The raw edges of the seam were turned under and blindstitched. Hand embroidery was added to enhance the seam. Embroidery worked by Hilda Wardell.

USING HAND EMBROIDERY

Make your blocks from the pattern of your choice, quilt them, and join them in the same way as the Dresden Plate Quilt described p.69. The variation is in the trim used. Instead of covering the seam with bias strips, you can cover it or add to it with hand embroidery. Plate 12 shows a photo of two quilted blocks which were sewn together and trimmed in this manner.

So that your quilt will be reversible, you should choose embroidery stitches that look good on both top and bottom, or — even easier — do not go all the way through to the underside of the quilt when embroidering. On the back of the quilt then, you will see no embroidery — just the quilting and a seam around each block.

70

It is a good idea to begin joining the blocks which will be in the center of the quilt first, then add on blocks around this nucleus. You will always be embroidering joinings which are on the outside edge of the quilt, if you do it this way, and it makes the quilt easier to manage.

USING DECORATIVE STITCHES ON THE SEWING MACHINE

Most of today's sewing machines are designed to do many decorative embroidery stitches, with or without attachments. This decorative machine stitching can be quite effective on a quilt, and it has the added virtue of making the joinings very strong and durable. Another advantage of this type of trim is that it is fun to do because there are so many creative possibilities with the various stitches available. Plate 13 shows a crib quilt decorated with machine stitching. Ducks cut from checked gingham were appliquéd onto white squares and outline-quilted by hand. Four blocks were seamed together, seams on top. A strip of white bias tape was then basted over each seam. A stitch pattern of swimming ducks was used on both edges of the bias tape to sew it down. Plate 14 shows the same quilt section on its underneath side. Quilts made by this method look good on both sides. To complete the quilt, quilt blocks were then added on around this section in units of two, the decorative stitching being done as each unit was added.

Decorative stitching can also be used to cover the block joinings without the help of bias tape or any other trim. The blocks are prepared and sewn together a little differently when this technique is to be employed. Directions follow.

When you first prepare your materials for making your quilt blocks, cut the filler square ½" smaller than the lining or block square. Thus, if your block size is 9", cut the filler 8½". The

71

Plate 13. Detail of "Duck Quilt" by author. Pre-quilted blocks were joined by machine and the seams covered with a decorative machine stitch by the Trim Method.

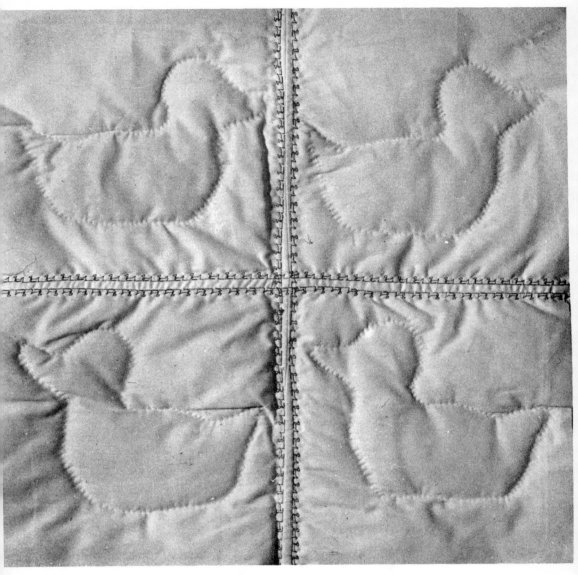

Plate 14. *"Duck Quilt" reverse side. Quilts made by the Trim Method are attractive on both sides.*

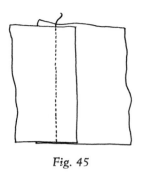

Fig. 45

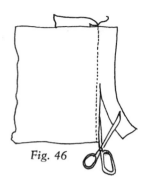

Fig. 46

Steps in joining two quilted blocks by the Trim Method

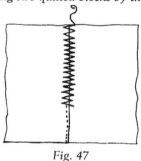

Fig. 47

block and lining will extend ¼″ beyond the filler on all four sides.

To set the blocks together, overlap the edges ½″, and stitch on machine down the center of this overlap. (See Fig. 45.) Trim excess from overlap very close to stitching on both sides. Leave no more than ⅛″ on both sides of stitching line, and less if possible (Fig. 46). Straddle this stitching line with a decorative machine stitch. Use a close zigzag type of stitch that will completely cover the raw edge of the seam. (See Fig. 47.) Plate 15 shows a kitchen mini-quilt which was made by this method. Two rows of machine stitching were used for extra width, although one would have sufficed. The bird was appliquéd and quilted simultaneously with the same stitch. A machine feather stitch was used to appliqué the bird's wings.

Plate 15. "Chickens," a mini-quilt by author, for use in the kitchen. The birds were appliquéd and quilted simultaneously with a decorative machine stitch, one block at a time. The blocks were then joined and the seams covered with the same decorative stitch.

USING BRAIDS, RIBBONS, RICKRACK, AND OTHER TRIMS

There are so many beautiful laces, braids, and novelty trims available at notions counters everywhere that it is easy to plan a quilt around one of these findings. Be sure the trim selected is colorfast, and preshrink it if necessary. Here are a few specific design ideas.

QUILT FOR:	FABRIC:	TRIM:
baby	blue or pink cotton with bunny embroidered or appliquéd on each five-inch block	blue or pink bias tape
girl	pink silk or nylon rosebud print	white lace
	yellow checked gingham	yellow double ruffle
boy	blue denim	red braid
	animal print	matching woven tape
woman	pastel print	blue or green velvet ribbon
man	dark brown linen or piqué	jumbo white rickrack or calico print bias tape

4

Triangular Puff Method

Puff quilts (Plate 16) are among the favorites of quilt-as-you-go fans, probably because they are easy to make and there are numerous quilt patterns that can be made up by this method. Many traditional quilt patterns are based on the use of a triangle to form the design, such as Yankee Puzzle, Old Maid's Puzzle, Brown Goose, and Fly Foot. (See Fig. 48.) The Triangular Puff Method can be used to make any of these quilts because it is also based upon the use of the triangle. In fact, almost any quilt designed around a triangle or square can be made by this method. Some suggestions for arrangement of the triangles are sketched at the end of this chapter.

Each block in a quilt made by this method is a square which has been folded into a triangle. Before folding, sheet wadding or other filler is laid on the square and edges of the square are turned. The square is then folded and the edges are sewn together.

Plate 16. "Star Puff" block, by author. Quilted triangular puffs can be sewn together in many arrangements including this traditional pattern called "Variable Star".

The size of the triangular puffs to be made will depend on the quilt pattern you wish to copy. The puffs can be made successfully in any size from two to five inches along each side. You can even use two or three sizes of puffs in each quilt. As an introduction to this method, here are directions for making a crib quilt based on a four-inch square (finished size). The finished quilt will be about 40" x 50".

Fig. 48. Four traditional patterns from triangular puffs

Yankee Puzzle

Old Maid's Puzzle

Brown Goose

Fly Foot

79

CRIB QUILT

Step One. Cut five-inch squares as follows: sixty-four pink, sixty-two blue, and ninety-six white. Use a yardstick and pencil to mark off the squares on the fabric, and then cut. This gives a seam allowance of ½" all around. The finished squares are 4". Cut 222 four-inch squares of filler. You may use ½" cotton or dacron batting, a sheet blanket, flannel, or whatever you wish for filler. Dacron batting gives the puffiest effect.

Step Two. Cut a cardboard guide four inches square. Center the cardboard guide on each fabric square, fold ½" seam allowance over edges, and press (Fig. 49). Remove the cardboard guide and place a four-inch square of filler inside the square of fabric. (There is a shortcut at the end of these directions you may take between Steps Two and Three.)

Step Three. Fold in half diagonally with filler inside. Baste along open edges about ¼" from edge (Fig. 50).

Step Four. Using a short running stitch, quilt along open sides ⅜" in from edge (Fig. 51).

Steps in the construction of a Triangular Puff Quilt

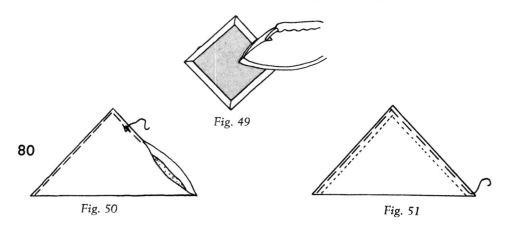

Fig. 49

80

Fig. 50

Fig. 51

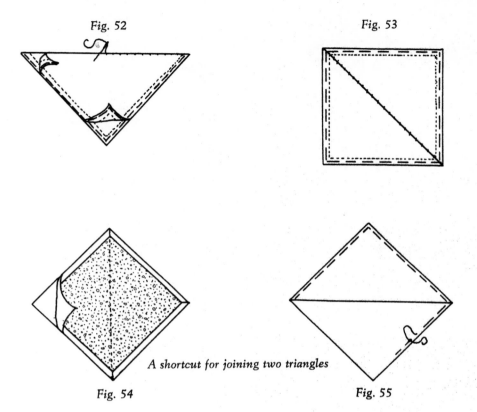

Fig. 52

Fig. 53

A shortcut for joining two triangles

Fig. 54

Fig. 55

Step Five. To make a square, place folded edges of two triangles together and sew with an overcast stitch. (See Figs. 52
and 53.) In this manner make thirty-two pink, thirty-one blue,
and forty-eight white squares.

Step Six. Arrange the squares in the color plan suggested by
Diagram I. Place edges of squares together and sew with overcast stitch. Be very neat and precise with your overcast stitches,
and when the puffs are flattened out the stitches will practically
disappear. Remove basting. You can see from the photograph at
the beginning of this chapter (Plate 16) how the puffs look
when sewn together.

81

= pink
= blue
= white

Diagr. I. Crib quilt made of triangular puffs

Shortcut. Here is a shortcut you may take between Steps Two and Three if you wish. Put two filled squares right sides together, edges even. Sew together with running stitch on the diagonal. Separate the two squares by folding each square into a triangle with wadding inside (Figs. 54 and 55). You now have two triangles sewn together to form a square. Proceed with the basting described in Step Three.

82

HOW TO ADAPT THIS METHOD TO ANY PATTERN USING SQUARES OR TRIANGLES

Step One. Find a pattern you like which is made up of triangles or squares of even sizes, such as 2″, 4″, 6″, or 8″. (It is probably too difficult to be worth the bother to fit together triangles which are of mixed sizes, such as 1½″, 4″, 5″, etc.) The Variable Star is a pattern at least 200 years old which is the basis of most of the nine-patch star blocks. This pattern is a good example of an old design which may be made by the modern Triangular Puff Method. (See Plate 16.)

Step Two. On graph paper, draw a picture of the block you have chosen. Each square on the graph paper will represent one square to be made of two triangular puffs. Designate on each triangle you draw, the color it is to be. Add up the number of triangles you need of each color to form the block. In the case of the Variable Star you would need 4 print, 12 red, and 20 white

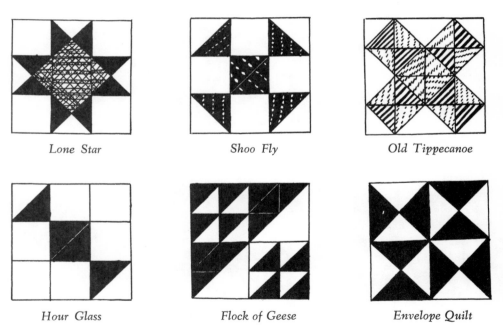

Fig. 56. Block sketches of traditional patterns based on the triangle

| Lone Star | Shoo Fly | Old Tippecanoe |
| Hour Glass | Flock of Geese | Envelope Quilt |

triangles. Make the triangular puffs and sew them together as described in the directions for the Crib Quilt above. Make the number of blocks needed for the size quilt desired. Join the blocks together with overcast stitches just as you joined the puffs together. Note that when all blocks are joined the quilt is finished. No need to bind the edges as when making quilts by other methods.

Fig. 56 shows some sketches of other old quilt patterns which can be made by the Triangular Puff Method.

5

Hexagon Puff Method

The Hexagon Puff Method is a modern adaptation of traditional English patchwork. It combines the Triangular Puff Method with the hexagon shape. The hexagon was used in mosaics on the floors of ancient churches in Europe, and it was probably these tiles which inspired its use in patchwork. Because the hexagon combines so well with the triangle and diamond to make a limitless number of design possibilities, it is not hard to understand why it has been the mainstay of English patchwork.

MAKING AN ENGLISH-STYLE COVERLET

Plate 17 pictures seven hexagon puffs sewn together to form one "flower." The coverlet is made by sewing a number of these flowers together. Each of these flowers is about seventeen inches across. You will need to figure out how many flowers it will take to make the size coverlet you want.

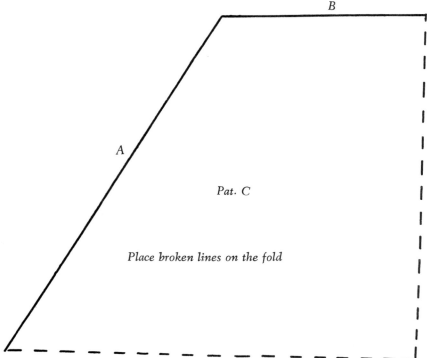

B

A

Pat. C

Place broken lines on the fold

Step One. Make a hexagon pattern by folding a ten-inch square of paper in half, then in half again to form a five-inch square. Trace off pattern C and place it on the folded square. Cut on lines A and B only and unfold.

Step Two. For each flower cut twelve hexagons of plain cotton fabric and two more of a harmonizing color. Cut seven hexagons of dacron batting which is one inch thick (or fourteen hexagons if your batting is one-half inch thick). Cut six assorted print flowers from pattern D and six flower centers from pattern E.

Step Three. Turn edges of flowers and centers under ¼″ and press. Appliqué the flowers and centers onto six of the hexagons.

Step Four. Sew one appliquéd hexagon to another plain hexagon of the same color, right sides together, in a ¼" seam. Leave one side open. Clip corners and turn. Make sure corners are well turned and sharp. Insert hexagon batt. (If ½" batting is used, put two hexagon batts in each puff.) To insert the batt easily, fold it in half then open up after it is in position inside the puff. Make sure batt goes into all corners well. Turn under edges of open side and blindstitch together.

Step Five. Hand quilt around appliquéd flower and center. Make five more hexagon puffs in the same way.

Step Six. Make one hexagon puff as above from the two shapes of a different color, but omit appliqué. A more elaborate quilting design may be used on this plain puff if desired.

Step Seven. The traditional English method for joining patches is used to join these puffs. Take two puffs and place right sides

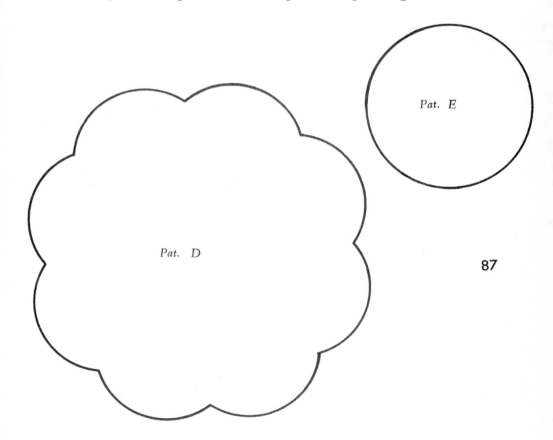

Pat. E

Pat. D

87

together. One should cover the other exactly. Use a fine needle and double thread, no knot in end. Take three or four backstitches on the wrong side of one puff near the corner. Beginning at the corner, whipstitch the two puffs together. Catch just two or three threads from each of the four layers of fabric. Push the needle in straight through all layers, not at an angle. Take care to sew from the beginning of one corner to the end of the other corner. Fasten with three or four backstitches at the end. (See Figs. 57 through 59.) Open out the puffs and finger press. If a firm tension has been used in the slipstitching, the sewing will hardly be visible. Join the puffs with the plain one in the center and the appliquéd ones around it.

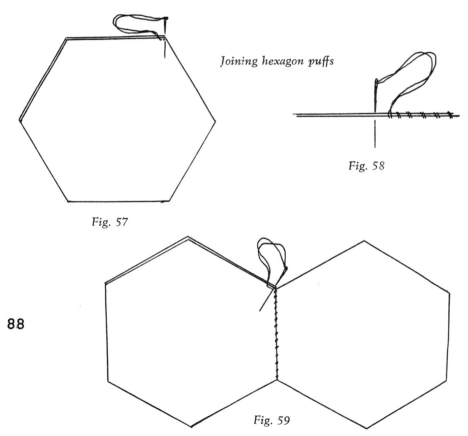

Joining hexagon puffs

Fig. 58

Fig. 57

88

Fig. 59

Plate 17. A "Hexagon Puff Flower" made by Grace Anderson of Greene, Iowa, shows how hexagon puffs look when joined. This flower is the beginning of a quilt which will grow as additional puffs are made and joined individually.

Fig. 60. *Arrangement of puffs for Hexagon Puff Flower Quilt*

Step Eight. Make as many more flowers as required for your coverlet and join them together in the pattern suggested by Fig. 60. Other possible arrangements for the puffs are shown in Figs. 61 and 62.

Fig. 61. *Quilt section showing another hexagon puff arrangement (The edges of both quilts may be filled in with half- and quarter- puffs)*

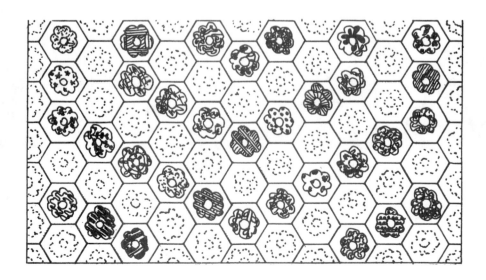

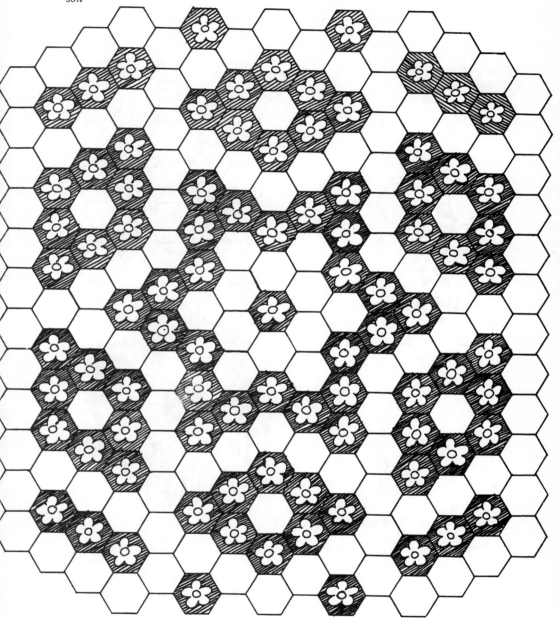

Fig. 62. Another hexagon puff arrangement, designed by Grace Anderson

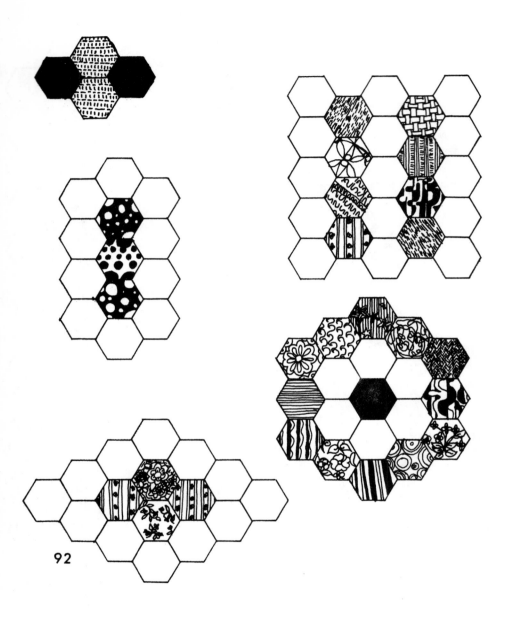

92

Fig. 63. *Traditional hexagon patch arrangements*

Plate 18. An American quilt made in the English style showing a traditional arrangement of hexagon shapes. Courtesy Lyman Allyn Museum, New London, Conn.

Plate 19. Another example of the versatility of the hexagon shape is found in this 19th century Canadian patchwork table cover. Courtesy of the Montreal Museum of Fine Arts.

The quilt is finished when the last puff is joined. There are no edges to finish, and the quilt is reversible.

Fig. 63 illustrates some traditional quilt patterns based on the hexagon. A typical English style quilt of the 19th century is shown in Plate 18. Another example of English patchwork is shown in Plate 19. Any of these patterns could be duplicated with the Hexagon Puff Method. Any size hexagon from one to five inches across can be used.

To plan a quilt using this method, draw a picture of it on paper, and mark on each hexagon the color it is to be. Make a puff to represent each hexagon in your picture, and join them as described above. When using small hexagon patterns, such as one or two inches across, pieces of nylon stockings may be used for filler.

Color Plate III. Quilted skirt, Christmas wreath, Christmas tree wall hanging, made by Marjorie Kerr from a design by the author.

Color Plate IV. "Bug-me-not" sign done in trapunto, large pentagon ball, patchwork pockets and belt on pants, Love pillow, checkerboard.

6

Block-by-Block Method

The Block-by-Block Method of QYG is one that can be used with almost any quilt pattern. It is equally good for pieced, appliquéd, or embroidered quilts. Even a very old pattern like Drunkard's Path can be made by this modern method, a happy marriage between the old and the new (Plate 20).

This technique is a favorite of traditionalists because it results in a quilt which looks just the same as one quilted on frames. The only difference in appearance between a quilt made by this QYG method and one quilted in frames is this: the lining of the traditionally made quilt will have one or two seams lengthwise and the lining of the QYG quilt will have seams around each block. These seams are not unattractive because they blend in with the quilting. Plate 21 shows the front and back sides of a quilt made by this method.

Hand sewing is the key to this successful method of QYG. The tops of adjacent blocks are seamed together (this seam can be made on the machine if you insist), and the linings of these two blocks are then blindstitched by hand.

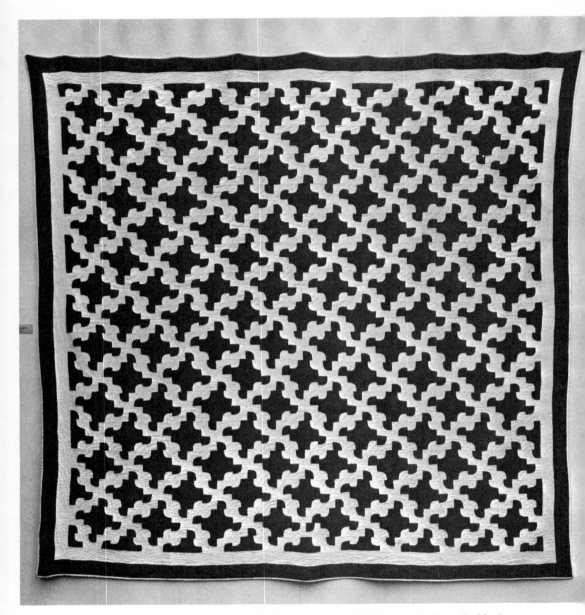

Plate 20. "Drunkard's Path," sometimes called "Rocky Road to Dublin" and "Fool's Puzzle." Pattern and instructions for making this traditional quilt block-by-block, are included in Chapter 6. Courtesy of the Denver Art Museum, Denver, Colo.

Plate 21. "Jewelled Chain" section by Pauline Campbell. This quilt is
a variation of the traditional "Irish Chain," but uses many bright prints
instead of the more usual combination of green and white. A look at
the back of this quilt (shown in the lower right corner) reveals that it
was quilted a block at a time.

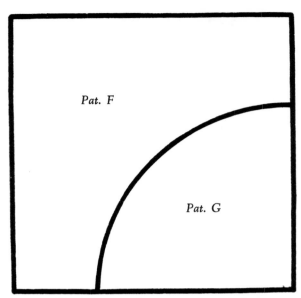

Pat. F

Pat. G

Allow ¼" extra for seams when cutting.

MAKING A PIECED QUILT

Here's how to make the pieced heirloom quilt Drunkard's Path the modern way without frames.

For a quilt 60" x 84" you will need thirty-five quilted blocks 12" square. Each block will be made of sixteen small units, each unit to be comprised of two pattern pieces, F and G. This quilt is traditionally made from just two colors, usually dark red and white.

Step One. For each block cut eight of Pattern F from red fabric and eight of Pattern F from white fabric. Also, cut eight of Pattern G from red and eight from white. Cut sixteen 3" squares of batting, and sixteen 3½" squares of white for lining.

Step Two. Make eight of the units with white Fs and red Gs; the other eight with red Fs and white Gs. (See the steps pictured in Plate 22.) Mark each unit with a quilting design.

Step Three. Lay a 3" square of batting on a lining square. Place pieced unit on top of batting. Baste all layers together.

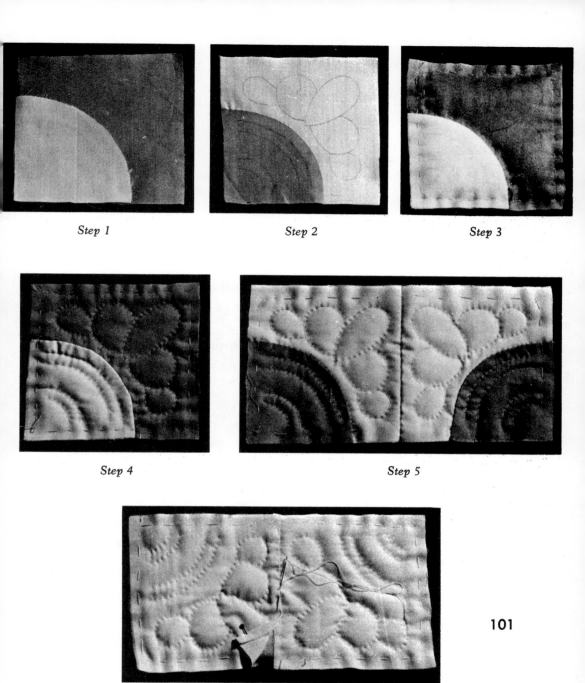

Step 1   Step 2   Step 3

Step 4   Step 5

Step 6

Plate 22. Steps in the block-by-block construction of "Drunkard's Path."

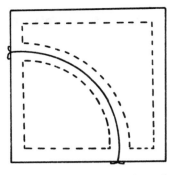

Fig. 64. Unit sketch showing simple outline quilting

Step Four. Quilt on marked quilting lines (see Fig. 64).

Step Five. Join two units as follows. Right sides touching, seam together one edge of the tops of two quilted units. This seam line should be precisely one-fourth inch in from the edge of the units. Pin the lining down out of the way if necessary. Notice that the batting will not be caught up in this seam. It was cut ½" smaller than the units so its edges would butt when the units were sewn. Open up the two units and place them lining side up. Where the two lining squares come together and the seam will be, fold back and pin the edge of one of the lining squares. Smooth the other square flat. You will notice that the lining square extends ¼" over the batting in the other unit. Baste this edge of the lining square down. (After you get the knack of this, basting this edge probably will not be necessary.)

Step Six. Unpin the other lining square and fold the edge under ¼". It will overlap the first smoothed-out block. Lay this folded edge down over the first lining square and blindstitch it in place, being careful not to stitch all the way through into the top of the unit. If your blindstitching is neat it will be practically invisible, and the seam on the lining side of the units will look like the seam on the top side.

Step Seven. You now have two finished, quilted units set together. Add on fourteen more quilted units in the placement illustrated by the block sketch in Fig. 65. You now have one completed block.

Step Eight. Make thirty-four more blocks in the same way.

Step Nine. Join the blocks in exactly the same way as the units were joined. (Substitute the word "block" for "unit" in Steps Five and Six.) Bind around all edges with a bias strip of red. The quilt is finished, except for your signature. Quilts are works of art and love, and should be signed. Embroider your name and the date in one corner, on either the front or back as you wish. Your heirs will be thankful for it.

Fig. 65. Block sketch of Drunkard's Path

MAKING AN APPLIQUE QUILT

Pauline's Bouquet

Pauline's Bouquet shown in the frontispiece is an original pattern designed in 1970. After the blocks are appliquéd they are quilted and put together in just the same way as the units in Drunkard's Path above. You will be working with 11″ blocks rather than 3″ squares as your basic unit.

For a quilt about 75″ x 90″ you will need twenty appliquéd blocks, twelve white quilted blocks, fourteen white quilted half-blocks, four white quilted quarter-blocks, and four white quilted border strips. The pattern pieces are all found on the following pages.

Step One. Cut twenty (H) from brown or rust, twenty (I) from gold, forty (J) from dark pink, forty (K) from lavender, sixty (L) from blue, one hundred (M) from green, and twenty (N) from brown. Cut sixty-four 11″ white squares, twenty-eight white 11″ half-squares on the diagonal, and eight white 11″ quarter-squares. Don't forget to allow for seams on these fractional squares. Of these squares and fractional squares, half will be for lining. Cut four border strips 10″ wide by 59½″ long, and four more 10″ wide by 93½″ long. Half of these strips will be for lining. Cut from half-inch dacron batting, thirty-two 10½″ squares, fourteen 10½″ half-squares, two strips 9½″ by 59″, and two strips 9½″ by 93″. (Note that the batting pieces are ½″ smaller than the fabric pieces with which they will be paired.)

Step Two. Prepare pieces for appliqué. (See Chapter 10.)

Step Three. Enlarge Pattern Placement Diagram II. Each square of the diagram equals one-half inch. Glue enlargement to piece of stiff paper 11″ square. Cut slits where indicated with razor blade or mat knife. You now have a combination quilting stencil and pattern placement guide.

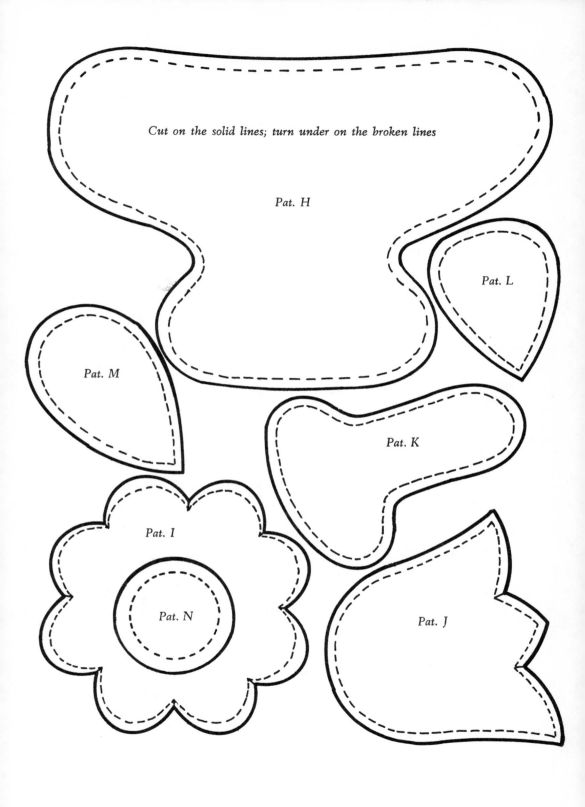

Cut on the solid lines; turn under on the broken lines

Pat. H

Pat. L

Pat. M

Pat. K

Pat. I

Pat. N

Pat. J

Step Four. Position stencil on one white 11″ square of fabric. Mark lightly through openings with hard blue pencil. Remove paper. Pin the pattern pieces to fit inside these markings. Baste pieces in place and appliqué. Embroider stems of flowers with one or two strands of green embroidery floss. Embroider stamens of flowers E with gold floss.

Step Five. Sandwich square of batting between appliquéd top square and plain lining square. Pin and baste. Quilt in short running stitches on marked lines around each appliquéd piece. In addition, stitch a parallel row of quilting around the outline of the flower and basket. (See detail of sample quilted block in Plate 23.)

Diagram II. Pattern placement diagram and quilting stencil for Pauline's Bouquet, (to be enlarged). Each square equals one-half inch

Plate 23. *Detail of the sample block made by Pauline Camp-bell for "Pauline's Bouquet."*

Do not let the quilting get any closer to the edge of the block than ½". If there is any "trick" to the block-by-block method, this is it. The quilting at the sides of the block (or strip) should be just ½" from the edge. This allows for the lining to be laid back and the ¼" seam to be taken without difficulty.

Step Six. Mark twelve plain white 11" squares with the same quilting design. Combine marked squares with batting and lining. Quilt these squares.

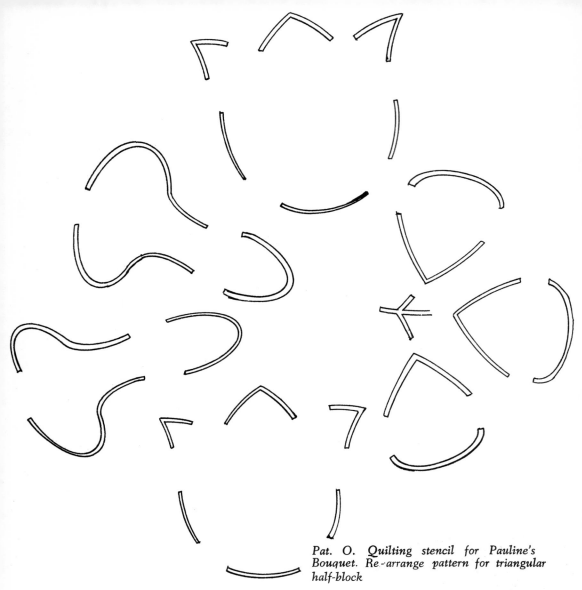

Pat. O. Quilting stencil for Pauline's Bouquet. Re-arrange pattern for triangular half-block

Step Seven. Patterns O through U are the quilting designs to be used on fractional blocks and border. Mark fourteen half-squares with Quilting Design O. Combine half-squares with batting and lining and quilt, adding a parallel row of quilting ½″ out from marked lines. Mark four quarter-squares with Quilting Pattern P and complete the quilting in the same way.

Step Eight. Mark the border strips with Quilting Patterns Q,

Pat. P. *Quilting stencil for triangular quarter-block*

Pat. Q. *Quilting stencil for border corner*

Pat. R. Quilting stencil for border

R, S, T, and U. See the photograph on frontispiece for guidance. Quilt border strips. Again, no quilting should be closer to the edge of any piece than ½".

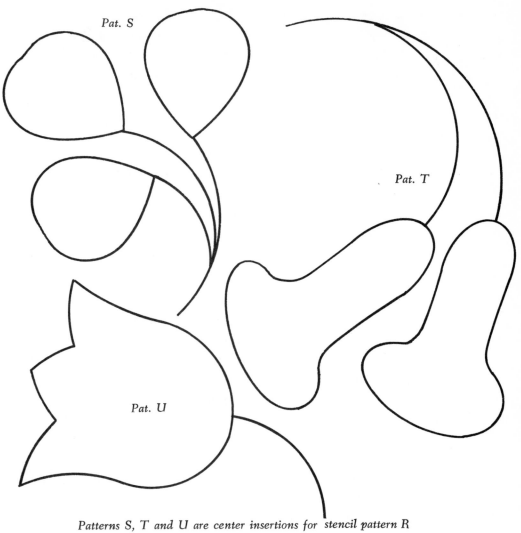

Pat. S

Pat. T

Pat. U

Patterns S, T and U are center insertions for stencil pattern R

111

Step Nine. Join appliquéd blocks to plain blocks alternately in rows. Join the blocks as the units in Drunkard's Path were joined. That is, sew the tops of two adjacent blocks together in a ¼″ seam, turn the blocks lining side up, and join lining squares with blindstitching. Join the rows of blocks together in the same way, and fill in the sides and corners with the quilted half-blocks and quarter-blocks.

Step Ten. Add on short border strips, one at each end. Add on long border strips to each side. Bind edges of quilt with white bias strip.

TIPS FOR SETTING BLOCK-BY-BLOCK QUILTS TOGETHER IN ROWS, WITH STRIPS, OR IN SECTIONS

Two blocks or units of four blocks may be joined together in the lap. Blocks which are being added to each other one at a time to form a row are easily managed in the lap also. Sit in an easy chair and enjoy the comfort of quilting without frames.

It is easier to join two large quilted areas, such as two completed rows, on a table. Smooth the first row out on the table top, right side up. Place the second row on top of the first row, right side down, edges perfectly even. Pin in place. Pin the lining back out of the way and join the two top pieces in a ¼″ seam. Open out the two sections, smooth and fold the lining squares in place as directed earlier, and pin. You may now take the work back to the easy chair and your lap, if you wish, to finish the blindstitching on the lining.

It is more comfortable to sit on a high stool or chair when sewing at a table.

Some quilters find working on a lapboard or tray is just as satisfactory as working on a table, particularly when joining areas such as quarter-sections, four-block units, etc. When joining long sections, such as borders to rows, the table is recommended.

A traditional arrangement for setting quilt blocks together is to use two- to four-inch strips in between the blocks. This may be done with the Block-by-Block Method. Simply prepare and quilt the strips separately in the same way as you prepare and quilt the blocks. Instead of joining a block to another block, you join a block to a strip to a block, and so on.

HOW TO FINISH THE EDGES

The binding of any quilt wears out first. For this reason, it is advisable to sew on a binding of double thickness. Perhaps the easiest and most satisfactory way to bind a quilt is as follows. Measure and accurately cut 2½" bias strips of one of the dark fabrics used in the quilt top. Sew the strips together end to end. Approximately one yard of fabric will be enough for the bias for an average sized quilt. Press seams open, and fold strip in half lengthwise with the seams on the inside. Sew the two raw edges of the doubled bias to the top of the quilt in a ¼" seam. This stitching should be done on the machine. Turn the strip to the wrong side of the quilt, and sew down the folded edge with a blindstitch by hand.

113

Plate 24. "1972 Flower Basket" designed by author and worked by Emilie Leman, age thirteen. The basket and five of the flowers were appliquéd before embroidering. The stitches used were chain, buttonhole, satin, seed, outline, Pekingese, spiderweb, French knot, straight, and back stitch.

114

MAKING AN EMBROIDERED QUILT

Modern Flower Basket

Baskets of flowers have inspired artists in every media, including those who work with fabric, needle and thread. The flower basket quilt pattern has countless variations. One of the most recent is the 1972 Flower Basket designed especially for this book. This pattern utilizes both embroidery and appliqué, a popular combination. (See Plate 24.)

Diagr. III. Enlarge diagram to twice this size. Each square equals ½".
Use black felt pen to draw pattern on enlargement. Lay 18″ x 20″
white fabric over enlarged design. Trace pattern on cloth with hard
blue pencil.

Plate 25. "Ilima" by Margaret Ahakuela, Honolulu, Hawaii. Courtesy
of the Ilikai Hotel.

You can make this quilt with the Block-by-Block Method in any one of several ways. You can make every block an embroidered block and set them together in rows to make any size quilt you wish. You can plan embroidery for half the blocks and repeat the design in quilting in alternate blocks. Or you can embroider a few blocks and set them together with quilted strips or sections as indicated by the sketches in Fig. 66. See Diagram III for directions for transferring design to cloth.

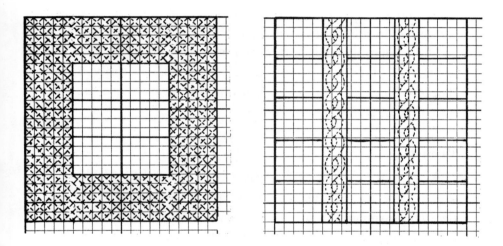

Fig. 66

MAKING A HAWAIIAN QUILT

To further demonstrate the versatility of this Block-by-Block Method, even the Hawaiian quilt may be put together with this technique. The majority of Hawaiian quilts are traditionally made of a single large design which covers the whole top. In Hawaii quiltmakers like to sit on the floor while quilting so the quilt can fall at ease around them. Many Hawaiian quilters use a large oval embroidery hoop, but others prefer to quilt without the hoop. However, many quilts on the Islands are also made in blocks. Plate 25 shows a typical block-style Hawaiian quilt, Ilima, which could be quilted block by block. The three-color strips and nine-patch corner blocks would be quilted separately and joined in the manner described above.

The mini-quilt made into a pillow cover, shown in Plate 26, is another Hawaiian pattern which would adapt easily to the Block-by-Block Method. This pattern was inspired by the Hawaiian plant Monstera (Pattern V).

Monstera

A quilt top 66″ x 87″ takes twelve appliquéd blocks 18″ square to be set together with 3″ strips. (See Fig. 67.) You will need approximately four yards of dark fabric (includes enough for bias binding) and eight yards light fabric (45″ wide) for appliqué pieces, strips, and lining. One quilt batt will also be needed.

Step One. Cut twelve 15″ squares from the light fabric. These squares should be accurate. On ironing board, fold one square of light fabric in half up and down, and iron in the crease. Fold the resulting rectangle in half crosswise, and iron in the crease. Fold the resulting square in half on the diagonal, and iron in the crease. You will then have a triangle of eight thicknesses of fabric, each crease matching and ironed flat (Fig. 68).

Place the pattern on the ironed triangle of fabric, matching the piko point of the pattern with the folded point on the fabric triangle. Pin well. Cut out around the pattern on the cutting line. Do not cut on the fold lines. Repeat with the remaining eleven squares of light fabric.

Step Two. Cut twelve 18½″ squares from the dark fabric. Fold and iron in the same manner, but do not cut.

Step Three. Unfold one dark square and one flower which has been cut. Carefully pat out the flower on the dark fabric square, matching the crease lines. Be careful not to stretch the flower. Pin in place. Baste.

Fig. 67. *Chart for Monstera Quilt*

Fig. 68. *How to fold the cloth before cutting*

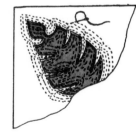

Fig. 69. *Quilting suggestion for Monstera*

Step Four. Appliqué the flower to the background, turning under the edges as you go. Use the blindstitch. Make eleven more blocks in the same way.

Step Five. Cut twelve 18½″ squares from the light fabric for the lining blocks. Cut twelve 18″ squares from the batt for filler.

Step Six. Sandwich a filler square between a lining square and an appliquéd block. Pin and baste. Outline quilt two or three rows inside and outside the appliquéd piece (Fig. 69).

Step Seven. Prepare and quilt the remaining eleven blocks in the same way.

Step Eight. Cut thirty-two strips of light fabric 3½″ x 18½″ and ten strips 3½″ x 66½″. Cut sixteen strips of filler from the batt 3″ x 18″ and five strips 3″ x 66″. Sandwich a filler strip between two fabric strips. Pin and baste. Quilt with crisscross quilting, the small leaf shape from the Monstera pattern, or any quilting design you choose. When all quilting is finished you will have sixteen short strips and five long strips.

Step Nine. Join the strips to the blocks by the method described earlier in this chapter.

Step Ten. Bind the edges of the quilt with bias strips cut from the same dark fabric as the background.

Pat. V. This full-size pattern for Monstera is in two sections. Super-impose dark line B on dark line A to join the sections.

A

B

Piko Point

121

Plate 26. "Monstera" by author, owned by Vivienne Jarvis of Honolulu. A pink monstera blossom was appliquéd on a purple background and outline quilted. Hawaiian quilt block patterns make interesting pillow tops. Photograph by Florence Haslett.

7

Quilting on the Home Sewing Machine

Many women prefer doing machine quilting to hand quilting because it is faster. For some, the primary pleasure in doing a project is in the completion — seeing the finished product, and the sooner the better. Others, of course, enjoy the work for its own sake and to them the final result is less important. Fortunately, the art of quilting offers so many varied techniques that all quilters may be satisfied.

THE QUILT TOP

Although some quiltmakers do not care for machine quilting they do not object to the use of the sewing machine in making the quilt top. If you are making a pieced top, machine sewing does make for a stronger, more durable quilt. A general rule of thumb is, if the pattern pieces to be sewn are three inches or more in any dimension they may be successfully sewn on the

Plate 27. Modern print, machine quilted by Donna Renshaw, Los Altos, Calif., together with some fabrics that would make satisfactory quilt tops for machine quilting.

machine. Obviously, it is easier to sew large straight pieces on the machine than small curved ones. (Some traditional patterns which call for many small pieces are easier to make by hand.)

Some modern fabrics may be used for a top just as they come from the store. These fabrics offer a good approach for a beginning quilter. All that is necessary to enjoy making a quilt is to buy the necessary yardage, line it, fill it with batting, and quilt it. Plate 27 shows one such fabric machine quilted and made into a child's quilt, as well as several other fabrics which would be suitable for quilts.

MACHINE APPLIQUE

Machine appliqué is fun and quick to do, and as sewing machines have improved so has the quality of the appliqué product one may expect. New iron-on interfacings, such as Pelomite or Stitch-Witchery, also improve the appearance of machine appliqué and make fabrics easier to handle. These materials prevent raveling, so no turning under of the edges is necessary. They also tend to eliminate slipping of the fabric and give it more body. Follow the directions that come with these interfacings and bond them to your fabric before cutting out the appliqué pieces.

The one thing to keep in mind about machine appliqué is that it should be simple. The lines of the pattern pieces should be straight or gently curved for best results. An appliqué pattern that has many tiny pieces of various shapes is better done by hand.

The charm of machine appliqué seems particularly appropriate **125** to children's quilts. The ducks pictured in Plate 13 were appliquéd on with a pattern stitch by machine. Some of the newer

Plate 28. "Rose and Rosebud" design, machine appliquéd and quilted at the same time, by author.

machines have stitches which look like the hand buttonhole stitch or feather stitch. The wings of the birds in Plate 15 were appliquéd on with one of these pattern stitches.

Some designs lend themselves to simultaneous appliqué and quilting. Such a design is the Rose and Rosebud made into a sample block (Plate 28). The flowers are simply free form pieces of fabric, and the detail which makes them look roselike is machine zigzag stitching. Four layers — the appliqué pieces, the top of the block, the batting, and the lining — were all pinned together, and the appliqué and quilting were done at the same time. The Ships-A-Sailing Wall Hanging in Plate 29 was also done by this method. This mini-quilt could be made into a crib

Plate 29. "Ships-A-Sailing," wall hanging by author, another example of simultaneous appliqué and quilting.

or youth quilt by setting several blocks like this one together with white strips in between.

When doing appliqué and quilting simultaneously, it is advisable to work with small sections or individual blocks. These blocks may then be joined by one of the methods described in this book.

Plate 30. "Instant Patchwork" detail, made by author. Zigzag machine stitching lets you patch and quilt at the same time.

INSTANT PATCHWORK

"Instant Patchwork" is another type of machine needlework that is interesting and fun to do. (See Plate 30.) It is difficult to categorize this particular technique, since it is a combination of appliqué, piece-work and quilting.

Step One. Measure square of lining fabric the size of the block desired and add one inch extra around all sides when cutting. This extra allowance enables the machine stitching to be started more smoothly. It can be cut off later.

Step Two. On top of the lining place a square of batting which is cut one inch smaller all around than the lining.

Step Three. Pin 4" squares of fabric on the batting, overlapping them about ⅛ inch. Pin each square securely. Cover the overlap with a close satin stitch on the machine. Cover the edges of the squares vertically, then horizontally. The block is quilted as it is constructed.

You can make block-size sections, width-of-the-bed strips, or whatever area you wish by this method. If you wish to join two sections, you may do it by the same method as described in Chapter 3 in the section entitled "Using decorative stitches on the sewing machine". Another way to join two sections is to trim edges all around so they are straight and true. Butt the edges of the sections over a piece of paper. Pin the sections carefully to the paper so they don't slip. Straddle the raw edges with a wide satin stitch. Be careful that both sections are always under the needle. When sewing is finished, simply tear away the paper. The joining of the two sections looks just the same as the joining of the patches. The quilt in Plate 30 is made of two sections joined by this latter method. Can you tell where the two sections come together? It is the middle vertical seam.

QUILTING EACH BLOCK SEPARATELY

Perhaps the easiest, most foolproof method of machine quilting is to do it a block at a time. It is like child's play to machine quilt an area no larger than twelve or fourteen inches square. Even curved quilting designs can be easily handled in this space. Traditional quilt patterns using squares and triangles make a good starting point for beginners, however, because they can be quilted in straight lines. Fig. 70 illustrates how six old favorites could be machine quilted directly over the seam lines.

When machine quilting individual blocks, remember these two tips: (1) Do not quilt closer than ½" to the edge of the block. You will need this ½" to work in when joining the blocks together. (2) Backstitch one or two stitches when beginning and ending each row of quilting so it will not unravel.

These machine quilted blocks can be joined invisibly with the Block-by-Block Method described in Chapter 6.

It is also possible to join these blocks by the Trim Method referred to in Chapter 3, with bias tape being used as the trim. If this method is chosen, it is suggested that the blocks be sewn together so the seam is on the wrong side of the quilt; then the bias tape could be handsewn over this seam. Bias tape used on the top of a traditional pieced quilt would tend to distract from the pattern itself.

Fig. 70. Sketches of traditional patterns showing how they might be machine quilted in straight lines.

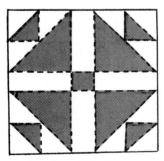

Duck and Ducklings

Cats and Mice

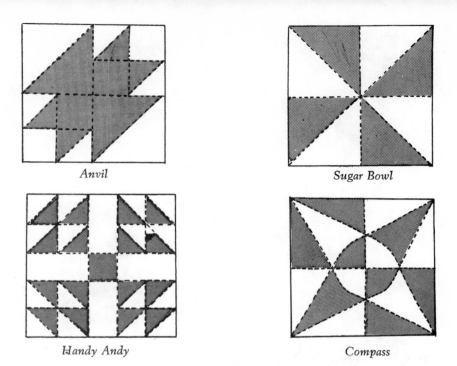

Anvil

Sugar Bowl

Handy Andy

Compass

QUILTING IN SECTIONS

Quilts may also be easily handled on the machine in sections. Plate 31 shows a modern quilt made by this method. Each section is quilted individually, then the sections can be joined by whichever method you prefer. Each section of this Tri-color Quilt is a 36″ width of cotton two yards long. This makes a quilt 108″ x 72″. The fabric for the top of each section was folded in half lengthwise and in half again crosswise. The fabric was then ironed. The resultant creases were used as guides in marking the quilting design. The design in the center was based on a thirteen inch square connecting the crosswise and lengthwise creases. A yardstick was used to mark parallel rows inside the square. The yardstick was then laid along one side of the lengthwise creases, and rows of quilting were marked parallel to the fabric's edge. This design was very easy to quilt on the ma-

131

Plate 31. "Tri-Color Quilt" designed by author and machine quilted by Hilda Wardell. Three widths of fabric in red, white and blue were quilted separately, then seamed together. (On the wall, a mini-Shadow Quilt).

Plate 32. "Quilt of 2989 Pieces" by Ernest B. Haight, David City, Nebr. Both the piecing of the top and the quilting were done on the sewing machine by Mr. Haight. His quilting method is described in Chapter 7 and illustrated by Diagrams IV, V and VI.

chine, because at no time was there a great thickness of fabric to maneuver under the arm. The quilting was begun on the smallest square in the center of each section. After all squares were completed, the long rows were done beginning in the middle and working out to the edges. The tops of each section were seamed right sides together, with the lining and batting pinned out of the way. The underneath side was then finished by hand with a blindstitch, as in the Block-by-Block Method. Quilting was then added directly on the seam between each section. The edges were faced with white bias tape one inch wide.

Plate 33. "Twenty-four Triangles" by Ernest B. Haight using the method he developed for machine quilting the whole quilt.

QUILTING THE WHOLE QUILT

The whole quilt may be successfully quilted on the sewing machine in about twelve to fifteen hours with no special tools or equipment. Plates 32 and 33 picture two quilts machine quilted by Ernest B. Haight. Mr. Haight used the system of machine quilting described in the following pages, and has quilted well over 100 quilts by this method, many of them prizewinners.

The "trick" to successful machine quilting is in the quilting pattern. It is possible to quilt curved lines on the machine, but to do so requires that you change direction of the stitching by turning the whole quilt. This increases the danger of bunching or puckering. It is much easier to machine quilt by sewing on the diagonal or bias in straight lines. The fabric will give a little on the bias, which makes it easier to keep flat the immediate area being sewn. The quilt is simpler to manipulate and work under the arm of the machine than when sewing on the straight of the goods.

The quilting pattern in Diagram IV is the basis of the machine quilting method described here. This diagram is somewhat simplified for easier understanding. Adding more quilting lines may be necessary, depending on the filler to be used. Cotton batting should be quilted closely, with the quilting lines no more than two inches apart. The lines may be three inches apart if dacron batting is to be used. If you plan to use a sheet blanket as filler, the lines may be as wide apart as you wish. Therefore, on most quilts larger than crib size you would need to add one to three more lines between the lines shown on the diagram. These lines can easily be added. Just keep all lines parallel and the turning points in alignment. Try this: Beginning at the point marked 1 on the diagram, draw with a pencil another stitching line parallel

135

to those on both sides. Your turning points will be at the asterisks (*). You will learn how simple it is to add lines of stitching between those on the diagram.

To get an overall understanding of the marking pattern, it is a good idea to draw it on a sheet of paper. As you draw you will see that the quilting is done in a series of continuous lines. Diagram V shows the first continuous line A and its turning points. After just the one continuous line is completed, the quilt is marked in large squares. Diagram VI shows line A to which line B has been added. The quilt is now marked in smaller squares. As each continuous line is added the squares become smaller.

PREPARING THE TOP

It is possible to quilt any top on the sewing machine, but this method is not recommended for appliquéd tops. Straight line machine quilting is too much in contrast with softer lines and gentle curves of appliqué. The machine quilting looks much better with pieced quilts using squares, triangles, and other geometric shapes. Modern patchwork fabrics are also attractive quilted on the machine.

To get the feel of machine quilting without risking a valuable pieced top, it is suggested that you make your first machine quilt out of inexpensive yard goods. Your first practice quilt will make a useful utility quilt, and the mistakes you may make won't matter much. You will feel confident enough to use a pieced top for your second machine quilt.

Step One. Sew two lengths of yard goods together to make the size quilt you want. Press seam open.

Step Two. Following Marking Diagram IV mark the quilting lines on the quilt top with a hard lead pencil, using a yardstick.

Step Three. Spread the lining, which is the same size as the top, on the floor or a large table. Spread the quilt batt evenly

136

over the lining. Put the top on the batting, stretching it gently, and pin all layers in place with safety pins. The pins should be in rows about eight inches apart to hold the layers together securely. Safety pins are especially recommended because they will not scratch your arms while you are quilting as straight pins would.

PREPARING THE MACHINE

It takes just a few minutes to get your machine ready for quilting, but taking the time to prepare your machine properly is important to the success of your quilt. First, if yours is a zigzag machine, remove the wide presser foot and replace it with the narrow foot for straight stitching. Visibility is better, making it easier to guide the stitching along the pencilled quilting pattern.

Second, remove the breastplate with the slot for zigzag stitching and replace it with the breastplate used for straight stitching. Using the breastplate with the smaller aperture eliminates the tendency for the quilt to wedge against the needle as it penetrates the cloth.

Third, balance the thread tension on the bobbin and needle so the stitches are locked in the quilt, rather than on the top or the bottom.

Fourth, clean the lint away from the shuttle, and continue to brush the lint away every time the bobbin is filled.

Fifth, regulate the machine to make about 16 stitches per inch.

Sixth, move the machine out into the open enough to allow room for the quilt to spread out and move freely. The quilt is easier to turn if it is not hanging all the way to the floor, so it is helpful to provide something for the quilt to rest on. Moving a couple of kitchen chairs, a card table, or whatever is handy, up close to the sewing machine, is all that is necessary.

Notice on Diagram IV that starting points A, B, C, D, E, and F are marked. Begin quilting at the left corner of the narrow end, at point marked Start A on the diagram, and follow line A around and around, until you reach the point marked Finish A. Backstitch two or three stitches as you start and finish each section, and roll the corners as necessary to pass the quilt under the arm of the machine. Keep the top spread evenly in the small area which is being stitched. Concentrate on this immediate stitching area, keeping it flat with both hands.

Next, start quilting at the left corner of the other end of the quilt at the point marked Start B and follow as before to the point marked Finish B.

Remove the safety pins as you come to them. The quilt is now quilted in large squares.

Continue quilting by starting at point marked Start C, proceeding as before to Finish C. Go to point Start D, sew to point Finish D. Then do E and F the same way. By this time all the safety pins should be out. If you have added other lines to the marking pattern, proceed as above until all have been quilted. Straighten the edges by trimming, if necessary.

FINISHING THE EDGES

To bind the quilt, cut bias strips about 2⅜" wide and sew them together to make a strip long enough to go all around the quilt. (It takes about thirty feet to go around a quilt 80" x 96".) Fold the strip in half lengthwise and stitch the raw edges to the lining side about ¼ inch from the edge. Turn the quilt right side up, fold the doubled strip over the edge, and stitch it down on the machine with matching thread.

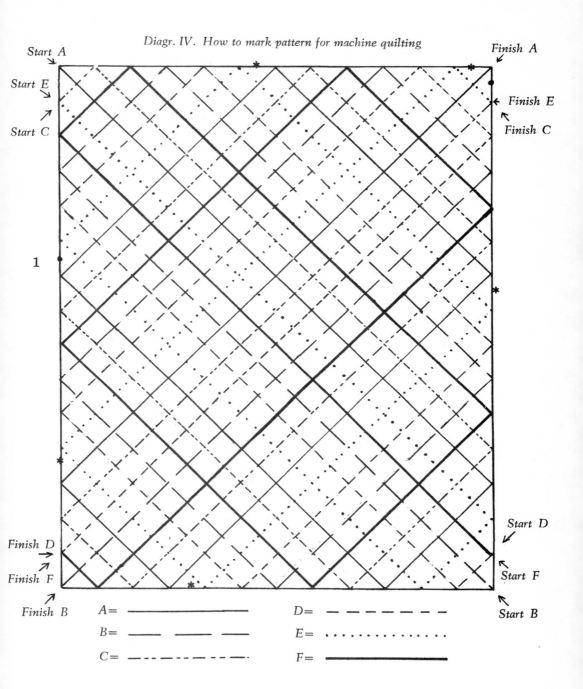

Diagr. IV. How to mark pattern for machine quilting

A= ————————————
B= —— —— ——
C= —·—·—·—·—·—·—·.
D= — — — — — —
E= ....
F= ▬▬▬▬▬▬▬▬

Start A   Finish A

Diagr. V.

Simplified
marking diagrams
for machine quilting

Finish A

Start A

Diagr. VI.

140

Finish B   Start B

8

Trapunto Quilting

Trapunto or Italian style quilting is a form of quilting which eliminates the usual filler. The quilting is corded. Almost any smooth textile background is suitable, although nylon, linen, shantung, and silk are particularly effective. A smooth plain fabric is best because the design stands out more. Trapunto is popular for bedspreads in warm climates, because it is not heavy. However, many more things other than bed covers may be made from trapunto. It is a beautiful way to decorate valances, vanity skirts, purses, eyeglass cases, pillow tops, robes, jackets, chair seats or backs, footstool tops, and almost anything the imagination can dream up.

This kind of quilting is done on two layers of material, with no inner lining. The design is made by stitching two parallel lines about ¼" apart through both layers of material. These lines form a narrow channel through which a cord or yarn is pulled with a needle, working from the back. (See Fig. 71.) The Love Pillow in Color Plate IV is done by this method.

Fig. 72 is a small design for practice which you can use to decorate an eyeglass case or a pocket.

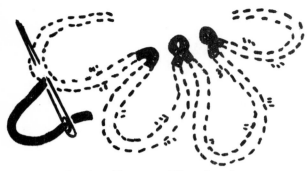

Fig. 71. *Trapunto. Thread cording or yarn, in between rows of stitching.*

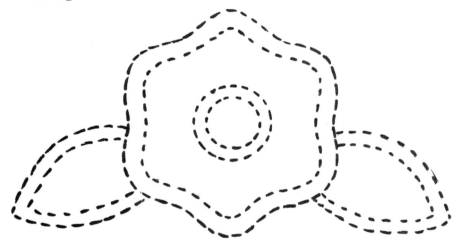

Fig. 72. *Practice trapunto with this simple design meant for decorating small objects.*

Step One. Choose loosely woven material for the backing, such as muslin or cheesecloth. Copy the design onto the backing material. Probably the easiest way to do this is to trace the design directly on the fabric. You may also copy the design by marking over the pattern with carbon paper between picture and backing. You could also use a transfer pencil and iron the design onto the backing.

142

Step Two. After transferring the design on the bottom layer or backing, baste the two layers of cloth together and sew along the lines of the design with small running stitches. Work from the back. If the stitches are not absolutely even on the front side, the imperfections will not be noticeable after the cording is done. As you stitch along the lines of the design, be sure to keep the width of the channel even for receiving the cording.

Step Three. When the stitching is done, insert the cording from the lining or backing side. Orlon or nylon yarn is best because it does not shrink. Use a blunt needle with a large eye to pull the cord through the channels formed by the stitching. Push the needle through the lining, between the two layers of material, and thread it through the channel. At each curve or sharp corner, push the needle up through the lining. Pull the cord through to the surface (the back side), and then reinsert the needle through the same hole or a little farther along. Leave a small loop of excess cord outside on these corners to prevent puckering. (See Fig. 71.) Continue the threading. Do not knot the yarn. You can insert the needle as often as necessary on the underside without marking the finished design.

The Wild Rose Bouquet design, Pattern W in two parts, is an adaptation of an appliqué quilt pattern dating from the 1920s. This pattern can be made into a pillow top, or used to decorate any item you desire. A silk or synthetic fabric in a pastel shade is suggested. Follow the directions above to make this trapunto design.

A variation of trapunto called padded quilting is quite often found in appliqué quilts. Additional filler is inserted under particular appliqué pieces in the design to give extra dimension to these pieces. Centers of flowers and fruits and berries are frequently padded so they will stand out. This additional filler may

143

144

Pat. W, part 1. Wild rose Pattern for trapunto

Pat. W, part 2. *Wild Rose Pattern for trapunto. Join this section to part 1, at the broken line crossing the stem.*

be inserted under the appliqué piece before it is attached to the background; or bits of filler may be forced in, from the underside, with a large needle or crochet hook. The latter method tends to damage the lining when applied to bed quilts, but it is quite satisfactory when preparing quilted fabric for use as upholstery, pillow tops, or other items which do not require that the lining be exposed.

This latter technique is quite effective when used on large floral prints. The fabric can be quilted in the usual way, with the quilting outlining the flowers, leaves, et cetera. Extra padding is then inserted under various portions of the flowers to accent them. Material quilted in this manner makes beautiful slipcovers or upholstery for chairs.

145

Plate 34. Detail of a quilt made in 1933 showing a combination of trapunto and padded quilting. The quilt is "Martindale Pattern," made from a pattern designed about 1840. Courtesy of the Denver Art Museum.

Plate 35. *"Autumn Leaf," is a copy of a quilt exhibited at the Chicago World's Fair in 1893. Bands separating the appliquéd leaves are worked in trapunto quilting. Courtesy of the Denver Art Museum.*

Another popular use for this particular technique is to make quilted pictures from pictorial fabrics. Fabrics suitable for this purpose are most commonly found in shops or departments featuring drapery materials. Find a printed design or scene that you like and buy enough yardage to allow for margins in framing. Quilt around the design features, using thick dacron filler (dacron is puffier than cotton) and a porous lining, such as cheesecloth. When you have outlined all portions of the design that you care to, insert extra padding from underneath through the lining. Spread the threads of the lining apart sufficiently so that you can poke bits of filler in with a blunt needle. Do not pad all parts of the picture, just those parts which you want to stand out in relief. Frame the finished picture just as you would any other picture.

9

The Quilter's Boutique

On the following pages are instructions and patterns for several of the mini-quilts mentioned in chapter 1 or pictured elsewhere in this book.

Some of the patterns call for quilted fabric. There are quite a number of quilted materials available in fabric shops now. Many of them make attractive substitutes for home-quilted fabrics. However, the variety of prints and colors is rather limited. Also, this fabric is nearly always quilted in diamonds or squares regardless of the printed design. Some prints are not enhanced by geometric quilting. Florals and circular patterns look better when the quilting outlines the design in the print. If you have a certain color or print in mind that you want quilted for use in making apparel or accessories, you may find it more satisfactory to buy the fabric and quilt it yourself. For small items you can quilt remnants on hand, either by hand or machine.

To quilt your own yardage for any pattern, just take an adequate sized piece of the fabric of your choice and layer it with ½″ dacron batting and a thin, inexpensive lining such as cheesecloth, muslin, sheath lining, or any suitable remnant. Make sure all fabrics have been preshrunk if the item is to be laundered. Pin the layers together and hand or machine quilt in the pattern or design you wish.

HOW TO MAKE A PENTAGON BALL

These fun-to-make toys are perfect for babies and toddlers. They are soft and light; and tiny fingers can easily grasp them. They can easily be made out of scraps on hand. Although quilted fabric is easier to work with, felt or any heavy unquilted fabric, such as corduroy, may be substituted.

Step One. Make a cardboard pattern just like Pattern X. Place the cardboard on either quilted or unquilted fabric and mark around it with pencil. Cut out the pentagon patch ⅜″ outside the marked lines. Cut out twelve patches in this manner.

Step Two. Machine stitch on the marked lines. This stitched line will be an exact guide when assembling the patches, so it should be accurate.

Step Three. Fold the seam allowance inside on each pentagon and baste, like Fig. 73. The machined seam line should be precisely on the fold.

Step Four. With a whipstitch just catching the two edges, sew one patch to each side of a central patch (Fig. 74).

Step Five. Join these five patches together making a cup (Fig. 75). Make a similar cup from the six remaining patches.

Step Six. Whipstitch these two cups together (Fig. 76), placing the points on one into the recesses of the other. Leave two sides open.

150

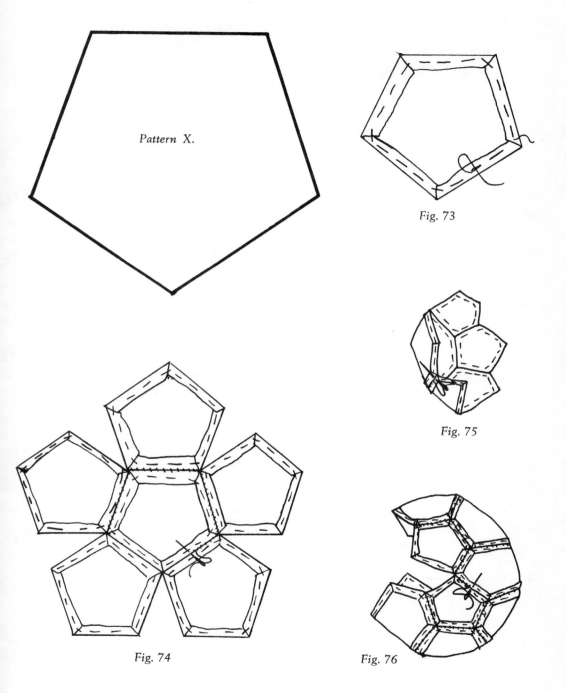

Pattern X.

Fig. 73

Fig. 75

Fig. 74

Fig. 76

Step Seven. Turn right side out and stuff with dacron batting or shredded foam. Ladder stitch the opening (Fig. 77). Ladder stitching draws the two edges together.

An alternate method which can be used with felt is to stitch the pentagons together with a zigzag stitch on the machine. No seam allowance is necessary, and the edges should touch but not overlap.

HOW TO MAKE A BUILDING CUBE OR PINCUSHION

Quilted cubes may be made any size you desire — small for pincushions or large for building blocks. They are constructed in the same manner as the pentagon ball, but the basic pattern piece is a square.

Step One. Make a square cardboard pattern of the size desired. Mark and cut six quilted squares as described in Step One of the instructions for making a pentagon ball, and machine stitch over the seam lines.

Step Two. Whipstitch the squares together in the form of a cross. (See Fig. 78.) Sew together the two sides marked A, the two marked B, the two C, and two D.

Fig. 77. *Ladder stitch*

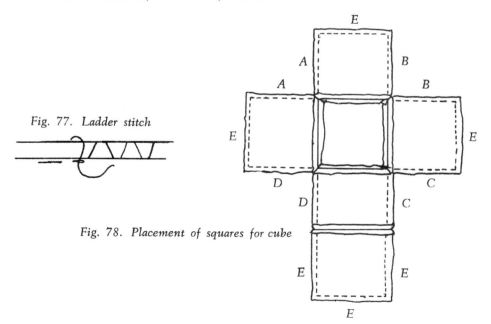

Fig. 78. *Placement of squares for cube*

Step Three. Turn right side out and insert a cube of solid foam. (You may cut a foam cube from a square pillow form.) Sew up sides E with the ladder stitch.

HOW TO MAKE A CHECKERBOARD

A checkerboard is made of sixty-four squares, eight rows of eight squares each. The colors are traditionally red and black, but any colors you like may be used. The finished size of the checkerboard is optional. If you want a checkerboard you can sit on or cover up with on a picnic or at the beach, cut the fabric in seven- or eight-inch squares.

After you have sewn the squares together for the top, and pressed the seams, cut a piece of lining and a piece of filler the same size as the top. Flannel or a thin sheet blanket is the best choice for filler.

Quilt these three layers together either by hand or machine directly on the seam lines. Finish the edges by sewing a facing to the top side, turn it under and slip-stitch by hand.

Flat buttons with large holes make good checkers for use with a quilted board on a motor trip. The children can store them on a large safety pin stuck into the board. Checkers for the large picnic board made from painted, plastic coffee lids are the right size, and they are lightweight to carry.

HOW TO MAKE PILLOW PINCUSHIONS

Miniature pillows used as pincushions make attractive accessories in the bedroom and bathroom as well as the sewing room. Made of elegant fabric such as quilted satin and velvet, they decorate the dresser or vanity, especially if holding jeweled pins.

153

One of these charmers may easily be sewn in an hour or so. Simply prepare two quilted squares of the size desired in any fabric or pattern you like. You might like to use two small quilt blocks, each quilted with filler and lining.

Sew the quilted squares, right sides together, along three sides. Turn right side out. Stuff with dacron filler, and hand stitch the opening.

HOW TO MAKE TOTE BAGS

One can hardly have too many tote bags. They make ideal purses for a mother going to market, or they make good diaper bags; they are handy used as shopping bags; they are useful as knitting bags, book bags, storage bags — you name it. Of course, they are always in demand as gifts, and they sell well at bazaars.

Quilted tote bags are especially nice because of the weight of quilted fabric. Quilted cotton seems to be just heavy enough so the bag holds its shape well, and it is very comfortable to carry. There are limitless design possibilities with patchwork and appliqué. (See Color Plate II.)

The bag itself is made from two quilted squares or rectangles sewn together. The seams may be taken on the outside of the bag and bound with bias. A second method is to sew the squares right sides together, just catching the outer edges and the filler in the seam. The lining pieces are then blindstitched by hand. (A further explanation of this method can be found in Chapter 6.)

There are a variety of ways to attach handles to the bag. A few of these methods are described in the following pages.

Martha Washington Star Tote

(See Color Plate II.)

Step One. Trace the pattern pieces for the Martha Washington Star, Pattern Y. Piece two blocks from this pattern. Sandwich a square of filler, either cotton or dacron, between each quilt block and a square of lining. Pin and baste the three layers together. Quilt directly over the seam lines, either by hand or machine as you prefer. Sew the two quilted blocks together, wrong sides touching.

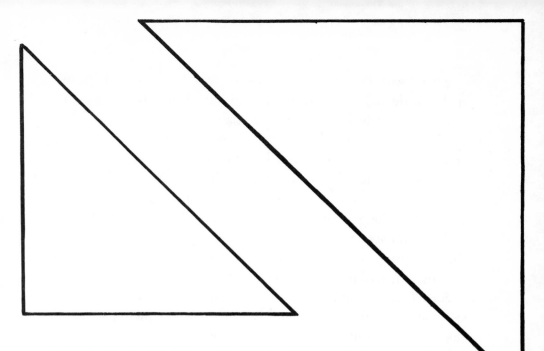

Pat. Y. Martha Washington Star block. Add ¼" around each piece for seam allowance when cutting.

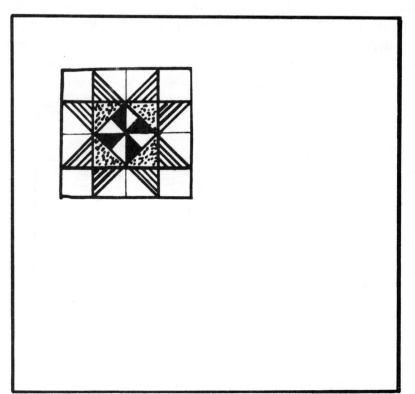

155

Step Two. Finish the seams as follows: Cut a bias strip, two inches wide and about seventy inches long, from matching fabric. Double the strip by folding it in half lengthwise. Press. Sew the raw edges of the bias along the seam line. Turn and hand stitch the folded edge of the bias to the other side of the bag. Save the remainder of the bias strip for the top edge.

Step Three. For the handle, cut two strips of cloth five inches wide and as long as you want the handle to be, about fourteen to eighteen inches. Sew the strips together on the long edges, right sides touching, using a ½″ seam. Turn right side out. Insert a four-inch strip of filler inside the handle. Quilt.

Step Four. To attach the handle to the bag, place it down inside the bag, right side up, and baste the ends to the top edges of the bag. The inside of the handle will be next to the inside of the bag. (See Fig. 79.)

Step Five. Bind the top edge of the bag with the remaining bias strip. Sew the right side of the strip to the right side of the bag, then turn it to the inside and slip-stitch in place by hand or topstitch by machine. Now bring the handles up in the normal carrying position. Tack the top of the binding to the handles by hand, or topstitch by machine if you prefer. (See Fig. 80.)

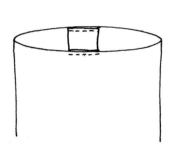

Fig. 79

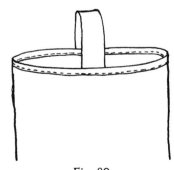

Fig. 80

Sunflower Tote (Color Plate II)

The pattern for this tote is a modern appliqué that was originally designed for a bed quilt to be made with the Block-by-Block Method described in Chapter 6. This bag is constructed in essentially the same way as the Martha Washington Star Tote, the difference being in the seam finishing and the type of handle.

Step One. Prepare two appliquéd blocks using Pattern Z. Quilt each of these blocks with filler to lining squares.

Step Two. Sew the two quilted blocks together, right sides touching. (If you want to finish the inside of this seam by hand, do not catch the lining into the seam when you sew.) Bind the seam with bias tape or finish it by hand. To finish by hand, turn the bag wrong side out, slip one side of the lining under the folded-down edge of the other lining, and blindstitch.

Step Three. Face the top edge of the bag.

Step Four. Prepare a handle the length desired by covering a cord with a bias strip. (See Fig. 81.) Sew the handle to the inside or outside of the bag as you prefer. (See Figs. 82 and 83.)

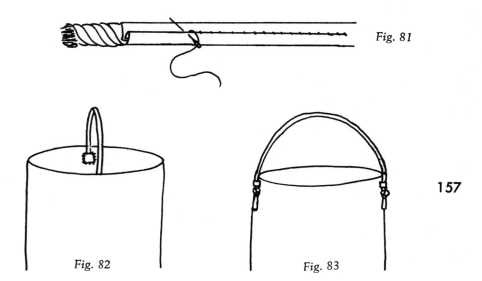

Fig. 81

Fig. 82

Fig. 83

157

Pat. Z, part 1. Flower for Sunflower Tote. Fine dotted lines denote quilting lines, coarser broken line is seam line, heavy unbroken line is cutting line. Place center crosswise line on fold when cutting.

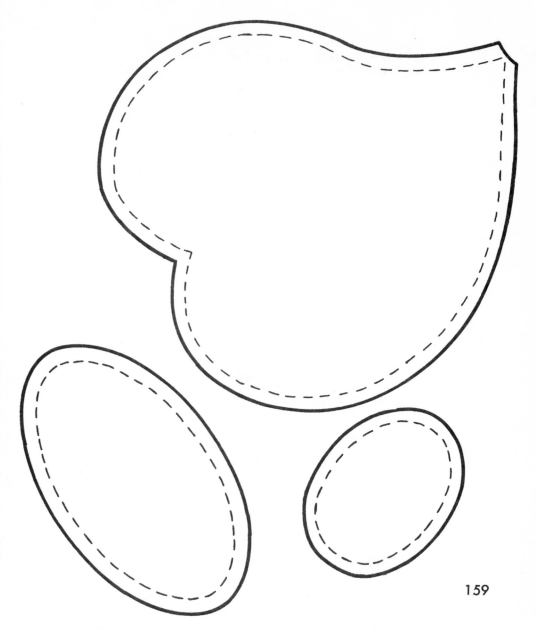

159

Pat. Z, part 2. Leaf, flower center, and bud for Sunflower Tote.

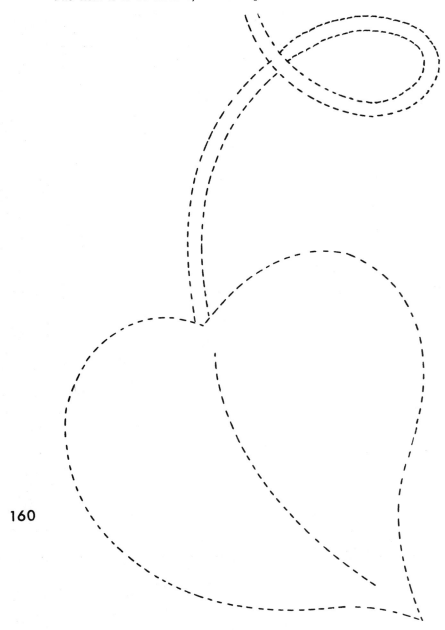

160

Star Spangled Banner Tote (Color Plate II)

This bag has a considerably larger capacity than the totes on the preceding pages, because of the extra depth given by the handle. It is made with two quilted blocks pieced from Pattern AA. After finishing the blocks, proceed as follows:

Step One. Bind or face the top edge of each block.

Step Two. Cut two fabric strips for the handle 2½" wide by 60" long, and one the same size from filler. Sandwich these together and quilt, making sure the quilting design does not enter the ¼" seam allowance on either side. Sew the ends of the quilted handle together. Finish this 2½" seam on the inside by hand.

Step Three. With the seamed ends of the handle on the bottom of the bag, pin the handle along one edge to a finished quilted square. Wrong sides should touch so the seam will be on the outside of the bag. Stitch in place. Attach the other quilted square in the same way.

Step Four. Prepare a 2" bias strip about 122" long. Double it, and press. Bind the seams and edges of the handle on both sides of the bag.

Any of these tote bags may be stiffened along the top edge, if you wish. Simply cut a length of thin wire, such as florists' wire, and insert it into the binding or facing, before you sew the last inch or two of binding.

Two more types of handles are sketched in Figs. 84 and 85.

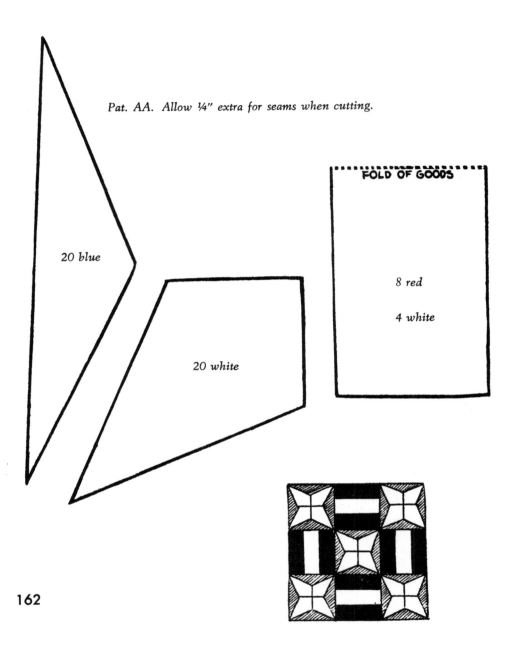

Pat. AA. Allow ¼″ extra for seams when cutting.

20 blue

20 white

FOLD OF GOODS

8 red

4 white

162

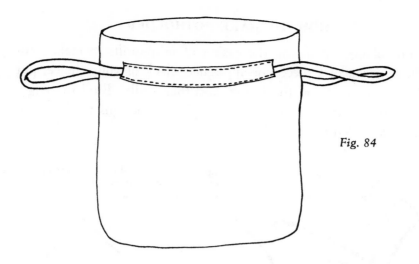

Fig. 84

Two types of drawstring handles for totes.

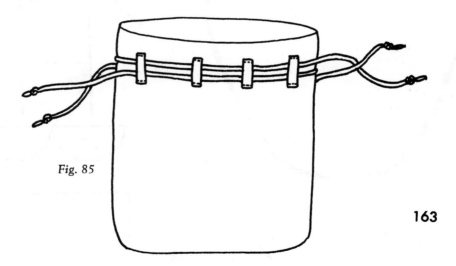

Fig. 85

HOW TO MAKE POTHOLDERS

Potholders are among the easiest of mini-quilts to make. All you do is make a pieced or appliquéd block of your choice, put filler between it and the lining, and then quilt. Bind the edges with bias. Patterns follow for the appliqué designs used on the potholders pictured in Color Plate II.

Pat. BB. Appliqué pattern for apple potholder. Add ¼″ seam allowance around apple. Stem and leaf can be made from bias tape. (Design by Florence Horner, Clarksburg, W. Va.)

Bias Trim Detail

HOW TO MAKE QUILTED PILLOWS

It goes without saying that pillows of every variety are popular. Whether they are better to give than to receive is a moot point. It is certainly enjoyable to make them, whether to keep, give, or sell.

Quilted pillows can be made any way you like. You can have quilted blocks on both top and bottom, or you can leave the bottom unquilted. The edges can be bound or corded on the outside, or seamed on the inside.

It is a good idea to enclose a zipper in one of the seams, or insert it in a seam in the back of the pillow, for easy laundering.

An alternative is to make an envelope closure in the back from two overlapping halves. (See Fig. 86.)

Ready-made pillow forms can be used to fill the pillows; or you can use shredded foam to fill a muslin case. Small pillows can be stuffed with dacron batting.

The corduroy pillow top shown in Color Plate I was made from eight 4″ squares and two 8″ squares. There were pieced together and quilted on the seam with a filler and lining.

The top was then sewn to an unquilted back made with an envelope closure. The pillow was turned and stuffed with scraps of dacron.

The Biscuit Pillow pictured in Plate 3 and Color Plate I was made by the same method as the Biscuit or Bun Quilt described in Chapter 2. Three sides of this pillow were sewn, the pillow was turned right side out, and a small pillow form inserted. The fourth side was then hand sewn.

The Moon Flowers Pillow Color Plate I was made by adapting the 1972 Flower Basket pattern in Chapter 6 (Diagram III). The pattern was reversed, and it was worked with appliqué instead of embroidery.

165

(Opposite)
Pat. CC. Cool Coolie potholder pattern, a combination of piecing and appliqué. Turn under edges of pieced figure to appliqué to background. Embroider features. (Design by Mrs. Elmer Leimkuhler, Harrisonville, Mo.)

Love Pillow

The current craze for the word "love" inspired the design for this pillow (Color Plate IV). A beginner could successfully appliqué this pattern because the letters are large and gently curved.

Step One. Cut a rectangle 14" x 20" from the fabric chosen for the pillow. Round off the corners to make an oval. Lightly mark a 7¼" x 12½" rectangle in the center of this oval.

Step Two. Trace letters from Pattern DD and add ¼" seam allowance. Cut each letter from the fabric of your choice. Cut a red heart and appliqué to "E". Turn under the ¼" seam allowance on all letters, baste and press.

Step Three. Position the letters inside the marked rectangle on the pillow top. If you like the three-dimensional look, stuff dacron batting under each letter. Baste and appliqué the letters in place. Go around each letter with a running stitch in black thread or embroidery floss. Mark the quilting design traced from Pattern EE.

Step Four. Line the finished top with preshrunk muslin or cheesecloth and fill with dacron. Quilt the marked design and around each letter as well.

Fig. 86. Envelope closure for pillow backs. Sew across each side of opening and seam to pillow front.

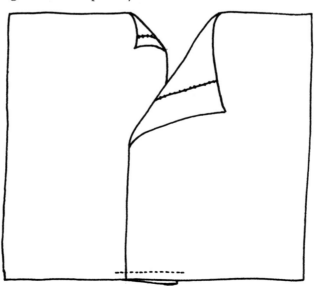

DD, *part 1.* Pattern for Love Pillow

168

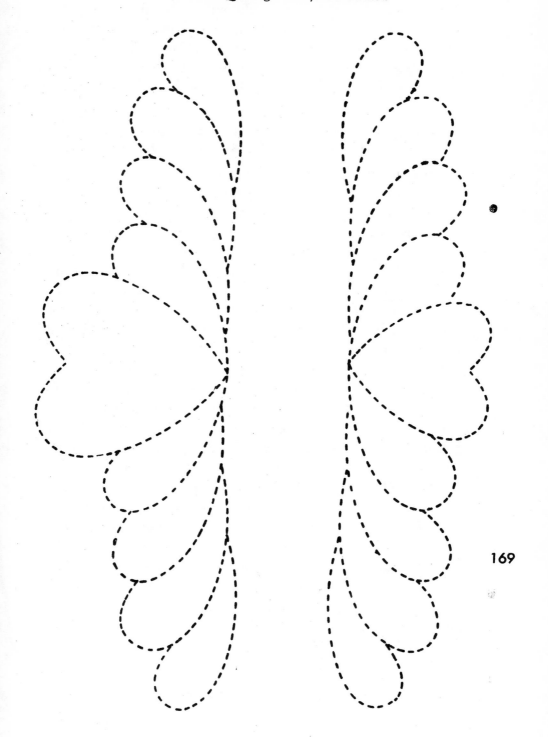

169

Step Five. Insert a zipper in the pillow back if you want the cover to be removable. Sew the quilted top to the back, right sides together. Leave an opening and turn, or turn through the opened zipper. Make an inner case of muslin, fill with shredded foam, and insert inner case into pillow cover.

HOW TO MAKE QUILTED ACCESSORIES SUCH AS POCKETS, BELTS, AND SCARVES

A quilted pocket, collar or belt made of bright appliqué or patchwork can make the difference between an ordinary ho-hum garment and an outfit that collects compliments. The hills and valleys of puffy quilting are irresistibly touchable, which may be the reason a quilted addition to a garment gives it such appeal.

Quilted collars and pockets are not harder to make than unquilted ones. In fact, they may be even easier because they require no lining or turning. Simply prepare the quilted fabric of your choice using ½" thick dacron batting as filler, and substitute it for the regular fabric when cutting the pocket or collar. Finish the outside edge of the collar with a bias strip before attaching it to the neck. The neck seam is made in the usual way. Any unnecessary bulk may be removed by pulling out the filler in the seam itself. All edges of the pocket should be finished with bias binding or tape before it is sewn to the garment. It may then be topstitched by machine, or hand stitched to the garment.

Belts made of quilted fabric have just the right body to hold their shape well, and they are soft and comfortable. (See Color Plate IV.) Simply quilt patchwork or other fabric, again filling with ½" dacron filler, the width and length of the desired belt. Cover all edges with bias. You may use bias tape, woven bias braid, or bias cut from the belt fabric. Add a buckle or closure of your choice. No eyelets are necessary, because the thickness of the quilting holds the belt in place.

170

Scarves are made like belts, except a thinner filler is more successful. One or two layers of preshrunk outing flannel used for the filler give the scarf just the right body and drape.

HOW TO MAKE A QUILTED CAP

The style of cap or helmet that you usually think of in terms of knit or crochet, also makes up attractively from quilted fabric. (See Color Plate II.)

Step One. Enlarge the cap pattern in Diagram VII. Cut six pattern pieces from quilted fabric.

Step Two. Sew the six sections together, right sides touching, taking ⅝" seams. Do not catch up the lining in these seams. Pin it back out of the way when sewing the seams.

Step Three. Turn the cap wrong side out. Finish the inside seams by hand. Smooth the lining from one section beneath the turned-under edge of the adjacent section, and blindstitch.

Step Four. To finish the edge, cut a 4" width of bias from un-quilted fabric twenty-seven inches long. Sew it to the edge of the cap right sides together. Fill it with a thick length of dacron batting, and turn it to the inside. Blindstitch.

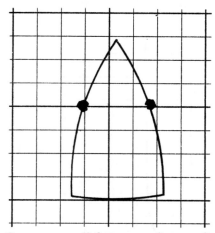

171

Diagr. VII. Cap pattern. Enlarge according to directions, in Chapter 10. Each square equals 1½". Seam of ⅝" has been allowed.

HOW TO MAKE A QUILTED VEST

A vest is made in much the same way as the quilted cap. Enlarge the pattern pieces in Diagram VIII. Cut the pieces from quilted fabric. Sew the darts. Seam fronts to back at sides and shoulders, taking 5⁄8" seams. Finish the seams as described above in Steps Two and Three. Bind all edges with bias. The fabric for the vest pictured in Color Plate II was machine quilted at home using nylon knit for both top and lining, and the binding was cut from the same fabric.

Diagr. VIII. Pattern for vest (to be enlarged). Each square equals 1½" for size 10-12 vest. Cut with back seam line on fold if you wish to make the vest reversible. Darts are optional.

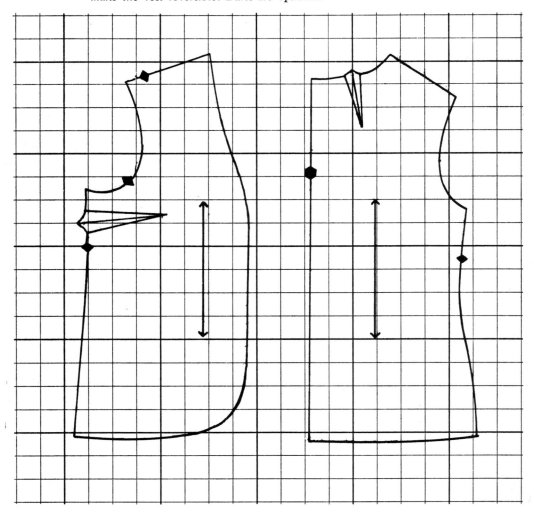

HOW TO MAKE KNEE WARMERS

Another fashion accessory perfectly suited to quilted fabric is the knee pad or warmer. (See Color Plate II.) They are so easy to make you don't even need a pattern. They may be made in any shape you like — round, oval, square, diamond, or rectangular. Decide on the shape you want and draw it on a piece of paper of a size to fit your knee, about six to eight inches from side to side. Cut two of these shapes from thickly quilted fabric. Make two small darts on each side to give shape to the pad. Finish the edges with bias, braid, or the trim of your choice. Make two elastic casings about one-inch wide from matching fabric. Insert elastic and sew to each side of the pads, adjusting the length so the pads will grip your knees.

HOW TO MAKE A WRAPAROUND SKIRT

Save the cost of a pattern the next time you want to make a long skirt for evening or at-home wear. This garment is extremely simple to make, particularly from quilted fabric. (See Color Plate III.)

If you are 5'7" or under, buy quilted fabric that is 45" wide. One width of this fabric will be your skirt length. If you are over 5'7", you will need to buy 54" fabric or add a border at the hemline.

The quilted fabric required for a waist measurement of up to 26" is one and one-half yards. You may wish to buy two yards if your waist is over 26".

Should you plan to quilt your own yardage, you will need to allow extra for the "shrinkage" or decrease in area that occurs in the process of quilting.

You will also need about seven yards of one-inch velvet or grosgrain ribbon.

Step One. Referring to Fig. 87 as a guide, round off the corners of your piece of quilted fabric. Bind all edges except the waist with ribbon.

Step Two. Sew two one-inch darts as sketched in Fig. 87. Gather the top of the skirt between the notches.

Step Three. Wrap the skirt around your waist and adjust the gathers to fit. The ungathered ten inches on each side should overlap in front.

Step Four. Cut two lengths of ribbon to fit the waist, allowing ½" extra for a ¼" turn-under at each end. Sew one length of ribbon to the underside of the gathered waist, with half of the ribbon extending above the fabric. Sew the other length of ribbon directly on top of the quilted waistline and the ribbon which is on the underside. The two ribbons sandwiching the fabric seam allowance will constitute the waist band.

Step Five. Sew on hooks and eyes to fasten. Add a ribbon bow, button, or other decoration to the end of the upper ribbon to conceal the closure.

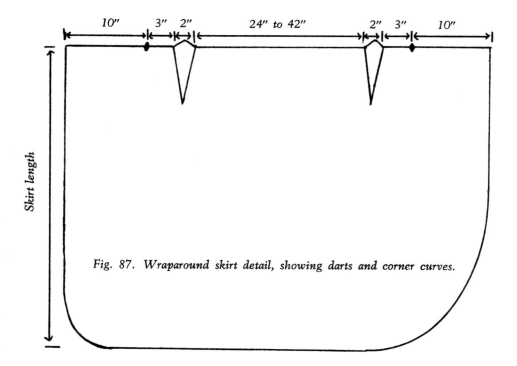

Fig. 87. *Wraparound skirt detail, showing darts and corner curves.*

HOW TO MAKE A CHRISTMAS WREATH

When you stop thinking of quilts strictly in terms of bed covers and apply your imagination to other uses for them, you begin to have many creative ideas for mini-quilts. One unusual idea is a Christmas wreath made like a Biscuit Quilt as described in Chapter 2. (See Color Plate III.)

Step One. Make forty-nine biscuits as described in Chapter 2 and illustrated by Figs. 1 through 3. Use four-inch squares of muslin, six-inch squares of cotton prints, and stuff with thick four-inch squares of dacron.

Step Two. Sew together two rows of fifteen biscuits each and one row of nineteen biscuits.

Step Three. Right sides touching, machine stitch three rows together. Sew the long row in the middle between the other shorter pieces, taking tucks in it as you sew in order for it to emerge the same length as the outer rows. When the rows have been seamed together they will all be the same length, the middle row having been eased to fit by means of tucks and pleats. When you begin to work you will see how easy this is to do. Don't worry about making a symmetrical arrangement of the biscuits as you sew. Small errors get lost in the puffiness of the wreath. The middle row will be the outer circumference of the wreath, and needs to spread to a greater length than the other two rows.

Step Four. Bend a thin wire clothes hanger to form a circle. (The hook will be used to hang the wreath.) Cut a piece of dacron batting the same length as the rows of biscuits and about eight-inches wide. Roll it into a "sausage". Curve the biscuits around the wire circle with the open edges to the inside. Insert the roll of dacron. Pin the ends of the biscuits together enclosing the wire hook. Turn under the edges of the open sides and pin together.

Step Five. Whipstitch the pinned edges together on the inside circumference of the wreath. Also whipstitch the ends together around the hook.

Step Six. Make a bow of calico to attach to the front to hide the hook.

HOW TO MAKE A PATCHWORK CHRISTMAS TREE

Another mini-quilt designed to give pleasure during the Christmas season is the patchwork tree in Color Plate III. Handmade decorations like this one can be used over and over again from one generation to the next, and the Christmas memories they evoke are long lasting also.

Step One. Trace off Pattern FF. Cut forty-five diamonds from assorted prints for the tree; three diamonds, two half diamonds lengthwise, and three half diamonds crosswise for the trunk; and one pentagon plus five triangles for the star. Add ¼″ all around the pattern pieces for seam allowance when cutting.

Step Two. Piece the tree diamonds together in strips of nine, eight, seven, six, five, four, three, two, and one. You will then have nine strips. Piece these nine strips together to form the tree. Piece the trunk from the remaining diamonds and half diamonds, referring to Color Plate III as a guide. Piece the star.

Step Three. Turn under all edges around the tree and the star and press. Appliqué to a 30″ x 50″ background of your choice.

Step Four. Line and fill the quilt. If you want a flat look, use flannel for the filler. For a puffy effect use dacron. Quilt, outlining the patches and the tree.

Step Five. Finish the edges by facing, binding, or cording. Attach loops or tabs at the top for hanging.

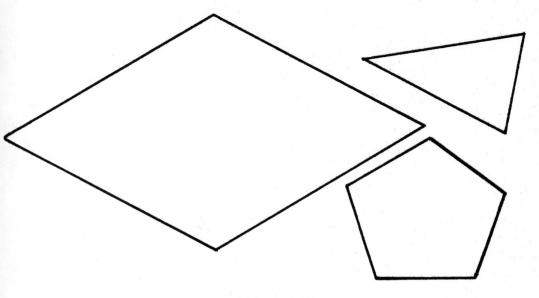

Pat. FF. Patchwork Christmas tree
Add ¼" for seam allowance.

10

What Every Quilter Should Know

HOW TO ESTIMATE YARDAGE FOR A QUILT TOP

The easiest way to estimate yardage is to figure how much fabric is needed for one block of the pattern you have chosen. Multiply the amount needed for one block by the number of blocks planned for your quilt. You then divide this number between the colors used for the pattern. If about one-half of the block is print, one-fourth is blue, and one-fourth white, buy the material in these proportions.

Lay the pattern pieces out on a piece of fabric to find out how many inches of fabric will be needed for the block. Don't forget to add ¼" per side for each pattern piece in the block for seam allowance, if your pattern does not allow for seams. As an example, let us take the Hole in the Barn Door pattern that is shown in Fig. 88. If you were to lay out this pattern on fabric, you would find that one block takes seven inches of 36" material. If you plan forty blocks for your quilt, you would multiply seven inches by forty to find out how many inches of fabric are needed. You would find you need 280". This number divided by thirty-six gets the number of yards, which is eight. Of the eight yards needed, a little less than half should be dark and a little more

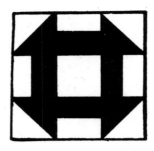

Fig. 88. Hole in the Barn Door

than half should be light. So, a good estimate would be 3½ yards of dark material and 4½ yards of light material. Add to this estimate whatever is needed for a lining, and for a border if one is planned.

HOW TO MAKE YOUR PATTERN

Quilt patterns should be made from something stiff and long-wearing which can be cut with scissors, such as cardboard, plastic, or heavy sandpaper.

Transfer the quilt patterns from this book, or elsewhere, onto one of these stiff materials. Cut out the pattern pieces on the seam lines. (Some patterns allow extra for seams, but it is better to make your pattern without seam allowance.)

Label each pattern piece with the name of the quilt and the number and color needed for each block.

Test your pattern for accuracy by making up a sample block. Many old patterns have been gradually changed through repeated tracings.

HOW TO MARK AND CUT PATTERN

For patchwork quilts place pattern piece on *wrong* side of fabric. Mark around the pattern with pencil, marking the exact size of the finished pieces.

Space the pattern pieces about ½" apart so when they are cut there will be no waste of fabric.

Fig. 89. Marking and cutting the pattern

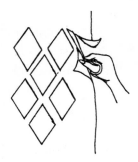

Cut ¼″ outside pencil line to allow for seam. Judge this one-quarter inch by eye, and cut pieces accordingly. The pieces will be joined right sides together, so you can see the pencil line on both sides when sewing. All that is necessary is to look on the wrong side of the cloth facing you to make sure you are running the seam right through the pencilled lines. This eliminates any element of chance in the fit and smoothness of the quilt.

For appliqué quilts the best way is to mark the pieces with the pattern on the right side of the fabric. When cutting, allow by eye for seams about ¼″. Turn the seam allowance under on the marked lines.

HOW TO SEW THE PIECES IN PATCHWORK

Patchwork is the art of sewing small triangles, squares, rectangles, and other shapes together so that they form patterns and designs. The success of your finished patchwork will depend on accurate marking and cutting, careful sewing, and the color arrangement.

Join the pieces together with a strong thread, No. 60. The thread does not have to match the fabric. However, if the fabric is dark you should use dark thread; if it is light, use light thread. Use a short needle, because you will be taking only a few stitches at a time and a short needle is easier to manipulate. Size 7 or 8 needles work very well. Sew the pieces together with small

181

running stitches. Secure each short seam as it is finished with at least two back stitches. It is also a good idea to begin each seam with two or three back stitches instead of with a knot. Seam the pieces on the wrong side of the cloth following the pencil line you made when you cut out the pieces. These seams should be ¼" deep, and sewed as straight and evenly as possible.

You usually piece the block together in one of two ways. (1) Sew the patches together which form each quarter-section of the block. Then seam these sections together. (2) Start with the piece which will be in the center of the block, and seam the surrounding pieces onto it. Add on around this nucleus until the block is finished. When fitting the sections together make sure that the corners of adjoining pieces match exactly. Tack the corners together with over-stitches if necessary to make them perfectly accurate. The sections are sewn together with the usual ¼" seam.

HOW TO SEW THE PIECES IN APPLIQUE

Appliqué is the method of applying one material to another by means of the hemming, running, whip, or zigzag stitch.

If using the zigzag stitch on the sewing machine it is sometimes unnecessary to turn under the edges of the piece being appliquéd. If the fabric is unusually ravelly, you may wish to turn edges under. Otherwise, use a close zigzag to cover the raw edges.

On other kinds of appliqué, the edges of the piece must be turned under and basted before being applied to the background fabric. After basting, the pieces should be well pressed. Place a hot iron on the cloth and press down — do not run the iron around the edges or back and forth since this may stretch them. Use steam if necessary. After basting and pressing, pin the appliqués in position, using fine needles instead of pins to prevent leaving marks.

182

Appliqué the pieces to the background with the stitch of your choice. This will vary with the design and purpose of your appliqué.

Most traditional appliqués were done with an invisible whip or hemming stitch. This is still the most popular method of appliqué. When using this method, choose a fine thread of the same color as the piece being appliquéd.

Another popular technique is to baste the piece down, then go around it with embroidery floss in a buttonhole or herringbone embroidery stitch.

The running stitch has become a favorite in recent years. This running stitch is placed about ⅛" inside the edge of the piece and is usually done with a contrasting color thread. The thread itself is used as a decorative part of the appliqué.

It used to be that to have your appliqué work admired, each piece had to be neatly, accurately, and invisibly appliquéd to the background fabric. In more recent times, however, creativity and originality of technique are more admired than neatness — at least by some modern quilters.

HOW TO ENLARGE A DESIGN

The most commonly used method to enlarge a design so that all parts remain in proportion is the "square" method. If the design is not already marked off in squares, make a tracing of the original design. Mark off the tracing with squares, ⅛" for small designs, and ¼", ½" or 1" for proportionately larger designs.

On another piece of paper (the size you want your design to be), mark off the same number of squares but proportionately larger. For instance, if you want to make the original design twice as big, make the squares twice the size of the small squares on the tracing. Thus, if the original design was marked off into

183

¼″ squares and you wanted to make the design twice as large, you would mark off ½″ squares on the second piece of paper. (See Fig. 90.)

Now copy the outline of the design from the smaller squares to corresponding larger squares. In this book the designs to be enlarged are already marked off into squares, and the legends give the size the larger squares should be.

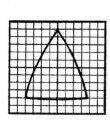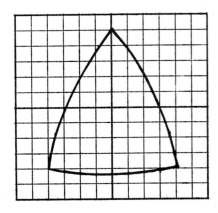

Fig. 90. How to enlarge a design

Bibliography

Anders, Nedda C., *Applique Old and New*. Great Neck, New York: Hearthside Press, 1967.

Finley, Ruth E., *Old Patchwork Quilts*. Newton Centre, Massachusetts: Charles T. Branford, 1929, 1957.

Harbeson, Georgianna Brown, *American Needlework*, New York, New York: Bonanza Books, 1938, 1970.

Hinson, Dolores A., *Quilting Manual*, Great Neck, New York: Hearthside Press, 1966, 1970.

Ickis, Marguerite, *The Standard Book of Quilt Making and Collecting*. New York, New York: Dover Publications, Inc., 1949.

Laury, Jean Ray, *Quilts and Coverlets*. New York, New York: Van Nostrand Reinhold Company, 1970.

Marston, D. E., *Patchwork Today*. Newton Centre, Massachusetts: Charles T. Branford, 1968.

McKim, Ruby S., *One Hundred and One Patchwork Patterns*. New York, New York: Dover Publications, Inc., 1962.

Timmons, Alice, *Introducing Patchwork*. New York, New York: Watson-Guptill, 1968.

Index

187

189